12.71

THE

rford, Ireland
616

200
WEB SITES
FOR SMALL
BUSINESS

The Top 200 Web Sites
CD ROM + Guides

This series of interactive CD ROMs with accompanying Guides provides access to the *best quality* business information sites on the Net. Forget those hours of frustrating searching. Now the work has been done for you. Illustra's team of researchers has spent countless hours scrutinizing thousands of Web sites to select only those that are truly relevant and useful to your specific needs.

Available so far in this new series:

- The Top 200 Web Sites on E-Commerce
- The Top 200 Web Sites for Marketing
- The Top 200 Web Sites for Personal Finance
- The Top 200 Web Sites for Small Business

Each CD ROM features:

- fast access to the selected sites;
- a fully featured Web browser;
- free online information updates.

Each accompanying Guide gives general advice on how to make best use of the Internet as an information resource, and detailed descriptions and ratings of each selected site.

Designed to save busy people valuable time and money, each CD ROM and Guide together provide a powerful interactive business tool.

THE
TOP
200
WEB SITES
FOR SMALL
BUSINESS

Sarah Lee

INSTITUTE OF DIRECTORS

illustra

KOGAN
PAGE

First published in 2000

Apart from any fair dealing for the purposes of research or private study, or criticism or review, as permitted under the Copyright, Designs and Patents Act 1988, this publication may only be reproduced, stored or transmitted, in any form or by any means, with the prior permission in writing of the publishers, or in the case of reprographic reproduction in accordance with the terms and licences issued by the CLA. Enquiries concerning reproduction outside these terms should be sent to the publishers at the undermentioned address:

Kogan Page Limited
120 Pentonville Road
London N1 9JN
UK

Kogan Page US
163 Central Avenue, Suite 2
Dover NH 03820
USA

© Illustra Research Ltd, 2000

The right of Illustra Research Ltd to be identified as the author of this work has been asserted by them in accordance with the Copyright, Designs and Patents Act 1988.

This book has been endorsed by the Institute of Directors.

The endorsement is given to selected Kogan Page books which the IoD recognizes as being of specific interest to its members and providing them with up-to-date, informative and practical resources for creating business success. Kogan Page books endorsed by the IoD represent the most authoritative guidance available on a wide range of subjects including management, finance, marketing, training and HR.

The views expressed in this book are those of the author and are not necessarily the same as those of the Institute of Directors.

British Library Cataloguing in Publication Data

A CIP record for this book is available from the British Library.

ISBN 0 7494 3268 3

Typeset by Saxon Graphics Ltd, Derby
Printed and bound in Great Britain by Bell & Bain Ltd, Glasgow

Sarah Lee is an experienced researcher and new-media consultant, and has published a series of articles on Internet use and business Web site evaluation. She has had her own small business since 1995, and specializes in how small businesses can make effective use of new technology.

Contents

1

Explore small-business Web sites with this guide

There is a large amount of potentially invaluable information available for small businesses on the Internet. Genuinely useful reference tools, company information, business resources and news sites abound, which business users will want to return to again and again.

However, most small businesses lack the time and resources to effectively explore the Web and locate those **genuinely useful** sites that are often concealed (let's face it) within a sea of **genuinely awful** ones. This guide is designed specifically for the needs of the UK business user. It will help you get to grips with using the Web as a business tool, by pointing you to useful sites, helping you become more Web literate, and making sure you get the most from your time on the Internet.

From this guide you can expect:

- Fast access (via the CD ROM) to high-quality Web sites of use to UK small businesses.

- A critical overview of business-oriented Web sites that are currently available online, and pointers that will help you become more Internet literate.

- A guide that concentrates on the **content** of Web sites and their usefulness to a particular audience, without being obsessed by the technology.

- Tips on how to get more from the Internet as an information resource.

- A guide that focuses on using the World Wide Web (WWW), although you will find a section on e-mail and newsgroups in each guide.

What you won't get from this book:

- A manual that will tell UK small businesses everything they need to know to become Internet experts. If that is what you want, put this book down now! This guide offers an overview of what information resources you can expect to find **on the Internet** in a particular subject area. The guide won't instruct you in the subject but it will give you access to a range of useful Web sites in your chosen area of interest from which you will be able to learn a great deal.

- Any pretence that every small business Web site that ever existed has been scoured in the process of writing this book. That's about as realistic as someone claiming to have catalogued and read every book in the world. Thousands of Web sites have been evaluated in the process of compiling this book, and every title undergoes the rigorous research process outlined below. We can guarantee that each guide features a hand-picked selection of Web sites that you will find useful.

- Detailed instructions showing you how to build a cracking business Web site, though we do include sites that may help you to do this. Our aim is to promote the Web as an information resource, and is therefore aimed at all business users who want to improve their Web skills.

Don't think this guide is going to stay up to date unless you regularly update it. We've all heard the clichés about a day being a long time on the Net. It's certainly true that what is currently available on the Internet of use to UK small businesses will have changed within a couple of months. Once you have bought the guide, updates can be easily obtained by visiting the Illustra Research Web site. Check it out for yourself by clicking the Illustra Button within the guide.

How we select and rate the Top 200 Web sites in this guide

Illustra Research has devised its own procedures to locate, select and evaluate Web sites, and the same criteria are applied across each of the guides in the Top 200 series. We have examined a wide range of methodologies that other people, often university librarians, have devised to judge the quality of information on the Internet, and have incorporated these into our own system. The editorial team has extensive experience of working with the Internet, and has brought this experience to bear on the process of evaluation.

All the reviewed and rated Web sites in this book have been individually examined and measured against our twin criteria, **relevance** and **ease of use**. We don't claim to offer a complete guide to the whole of the Internet, because no one can truthfully claim that. Instead, we use these criteria to present a shortlist of the very best sites our team of authors and researchers have found over months of searching and evaluation.

Our main principle is determining the extent to which a Web site meets the needs of a particular group of users. We are not trying to establish a universal quality standard, nor a 'Good Housekeeping seal of approval' system. We have designed our system of selection and evaluation to present sites that we think our target group of users is going to find valuable as information sources.

But can you trust our judgements? Doesn't any review or rating system in the end depend on personal taste? How can a star rating sum up the value of a Web site? Responding to these concerns we have developed a two step method for identifying sites worth sharing. Our authors have employed this evaluation process and we include details to show how demanding we have been when choosing the sites for the Top 200 series.

Step one: establishing threshold criteria

With thousands of potential sites to sift through we established our baseline for inclusion. Using our two criteria, relevance and ease of use, we designed a checklist of those attributes a Web site must possess before we consider recommending it.

Relevance

Here we think about the accuracy and credibility of the site's content. Is the purpose and scope of the site clear, or does it have a hidden agenda? Does the site undergo regular updates or revisions? Is there a physical address, or at least a phone number, to confirm the existence in the real world of those responsible for the Web site? Does the site present information in a way that is sensitive to what a particular group of users (in this case UK small businesses) is likely to want?

Ease of use

Here we look at the design and the navigation facilities. We consider how friendly they are for a newcomer to the Web – someone short of time but hungry for information. What is the general appearance of the site? Is the text easy to read? Are the links appropriate and well described? We think that interactivity is essential for an effective Web site: you should be able to ask questions, carry out transactions and generally use the information in a more active way that simply reading words off a screen. So the sites we rate highly offer much more than simply an e-mail address for communication with their users.

Step two: awarding a star rating

The star rating for relevance and ease of use provides a quick guide to what the site offers. Sites that satisfy the threshold criteria are measured on a scale of one to five. Here we distinguish what is good, what is better and what is truly outstanding. The key to the ratings is listed here in full.

Relevance

☼   This site offers basic information of use to the intended audience for the guide.

☼☼   This site provides some useful information plus some expert insight or value.

☼☼☼   A comprehensive site with authoritative information and resources.

☼☼☼☼   An excellent, authoritative site with features that make it an indispensable tool.

☼☼☼☼☼   The very best of its kind to be found at present. A 'must see'.

Ease of Use

☼   An accessible, easy to navigate interface with limited interactive features.

☼☼   An interface with some interactive features that enrich user experience.

☼☼☼   An interface that conveys a high level of design and usability in most areas.

☼☼☼☼   An interface that conveys a high level of design and usability in all areas.

☼☼☼☼☼   The best in its class, redefining the current standard of excellence.

A one star rating for relevance indicates that the site is well worth a visit for basic information, some of which may be unique to the organization that runs the site and will not be found elsewhere. As each of our guides is aimed at a particular group of business users, all the sites recommended in them have a value; if we have found a site that we think is useful, then it will be in the guide. For this reason there are no zero scores for relevance in The Top 200 guides – what would be the point? Some sites may have a zero score for ease of use however. In such cases the standard of information contained on the Web site exceeds or compensates for the poor design of the site. We trust that in time, perhaps even by the time you come to visit the Web site, improvements will have been made and the usability of the site will match the standard of its content.

Rapid change is one of the Web's greatest strengths as an information source and we appreciate that sites can alter between visits. We are committed to constantly reviewing and re-evaluating the contents of our guides. For this reason all our reviews carry the date the site was assessed. A site that is regularly updated and has satisfied our demand for accuracy, credibility and usability should, by its nature, maintain a high standard. But your comments and contributions are invaluable. If you think our reviews don't match your views, it may be because the site has changed, so please do let us know if you've found a site you think we should include – visit the Illustra Web site by clicking the Illustra button, then click on **My Sites**.

2

Using the Internet for business

So what's all the fuss about?

The rise of the Internet is seemingly unstoppable. Media coverage reminds us daily that the Internet and the Web are going to transform how people live and do business. We are urged to go online and get Internet literate. Bookshops are adorned with guides to becoming 'Net savvy'– but have you wondered what all the fuss is about? Have you noticed that using the Internet can be disappointing or even worse, a positively frustrating experience?

The Internet for many people is an **information jungle,** and the sheer scale of information available is overwhelming. Search engines offer a crude and inadequate tool for information searching, since no quality assurance system operates. Most searches made with search engines return a vast number of Web sites, with no guarantee that the information turned up will be useful or relevant.

Business users don't have time or money to waste doing this sort of thankless searching. What you need is access to high-quality Web sites oriented to the specific needs of a business audience. However, when you use the Web, you end up 'ploughing' through thousands of largely irrelevant search results; it's like being given an unreliable and gargantuan guide to the world when you just want solid and dependable information about a weekend break in Lisbon.

To make it worse, half the sites you come across are appalling, out of date or 'under construction'. How many businesses do you know who would mail out a sales brochure with blank pages saying 'not yet written'? There is no quality control or equivalent of 'refuse disposal' on the Web, and again and again you will come across 'detritus' sites created and then abandoned, filled with inaccurate and incomplete information. Using the Web feels more like 'grubbing around' in a skip than being on an information superhighway, and you can waste half the morning on unsuccessful Internet searches. So what *is* all the fuss about?

The value of the Internet to business users

Despite these familiar difficulties, there *is* useful information available on the Web, which *can* save UK business users time and money. For example, did you know that British business users can currently use the Web for all the following activities without any payment:

- Check phone bills and amend discount offers.
- Print out detailed street maps of anywhere in the UK by typing in a postcode.
- Set up e-mail groups, which enable them to keep in contact with business colleagues who don't share a computer network with them.
- Compare house prices, crime rates or council tax bills with those in other areas or with the national average.
- Compare water, gas and electricity bills with what they might have paid with a different supplier.
- Find businesses, UK phone numbers, UK postcodes, company information – all for free!

Apart from these 'business essentials' that anyone will find useful, (which are of course all in the guide) there is specific information out there relevant to your business. Whether you need to know about employment law, job vacancies, training opportunities, stock market quotations or export markets, there is often timely information that can be much easier to obtain than it is in print – provided you know where to look. However, it takes time and some degree of familiarity with the Web to locate these useful sites, and neither of these is easy for over-stretched business users to acquire.

The guide saves time and effort by offering an overview of a particular subject of relevance to business users, and by providing fast access via the CD ROM to some of the most useful sites in that area. Each guide is packed with reviews of Web sites that have been hand-picked for their usefulness and quality. The research is invaluable for beginners and experienced users alike, since the guides take all the hassle out of Internet use, with no more hours spent bleary eyed, 'ploughing' through hundreds of irrelevant search findings.

User driven, not technology driven

The solid research behind the guides is based on a clear under-standing of how the Internet works as channel of communication and information, not just as a technology. You will have already found that most guides to the Internet tell you more than you ever want to know about the technology, but less than you need to know about what is out there. The guides in The Top 200 series tell you how to *use* the technology, and focus on the specific needs of groups of users. For example, we know the Internet is good for British business users for the following reasons:

Essential business benefits of the Internet – a summary

▪ The Internet provides access to a wealth of up-to-date information from a variety of sources, which can be invaluable for businesses when information changes quickly, or when comparisons need to be made, eg for purchasing.

- The Internet is a cost-effective channel for communication, especially in global terms.

- It provides a good way to network and to generate business that goes far beyond one's physical geographic reach.

- It gives small companies the opportunity to compete on the same footing with larger companies since they can sell on a global scale without the large overheads of a shop front presence or having to embark on costly paper-based marketing campaigns.

- The interactive features of the Web can be used to create more sophisticated and attractive product delivery channels for consumers, eg through providing searchable databases on product lines or by providing links to other sites. This benefits vendors *and* consumers.

- The Internet offers access to free, good-quality information which cannot be obtained as easily or as conveniently from other sources.

How can good-quality information be free on the Web?

This is because many organizations have jumped on the online bandwagon but haven't worked out yet how to make people pay for this information. On commercial sites, revenue is usually acquired by following an advertising model, and because Web sites want to attract people to them, and therefore keep advertisers happy, they offer services and features including free information that they hope will pull in visitors. This might change with the development of new kinds of online payment systems, but at the moment it makes much of the free information on the Web extremely valuable – if you can find it, of course.

The other reason why valuable information is available on the Web without charge is that many of the information providers are governmental or non-profit-making bodies. They offer information as a function of their responsibilities to the public.

Why you shouldn't ignore the Internet

You may be bored by all the hype around the Internet. However, there are some important reasons why businesses should not ignore the Internet. For example, one reason why it is currently difficult to locate good-quality sites is that hype and excitement about the Web has led to companies and organizations rushing to 'get online'. Consequently there are many sites currently available that have no obvious value or usefulness and have been thrown up by companies desperate to carve out a Web presence for themselves. They are created without enough consideration or awareness as to what makes a valuable or useful Web site. They are usually ill conceived and poorly designed 'corporate brochures', so it is not surprising that their Web pages are frustrating to users (see Chapter 3).

However, as the technology matures, and the use and design of Web sites becomes more sophisticated, it is likely that many of the more hopeless sites will get 'weeded out', and Internet users will become more adept at recognizing styles and categories of sites. These more literate Internet business users will be significantly advantaged over individuals who have shunned the Internet because they think it is full of rubbish, and have yet to acquire any familiarity with it; or users like those TV viewers who don't recognize the distinction between soap operas and news broadcasts. Since the Internet is here to stay, some degree of Internet literacy is necessary just to be able to operate in the new channels of communication and information that have been created for business by the Web. Even if you have other people in your organization whose job it is to 'ferret out' the necessary information, it will help you considerably if you know what can be done with the Internet – and can judge for example whether that research really would take a week to complete!

Key points

- Don't ignore the Internet because you think it'll go away – it won't!
- Don't allow yourself to be swayed or panicked by the hype.
- Recognize the strengths of the Internet for business as well as its weaknesses.
- Use this guide to begin to make yourself more Internet literate.

How we deal with commercial sites or vendors

In this book and on the CD ROM, you will find reviews of vendors' sites in a range of product areas. These sites have been included because they are good examples of their kind, eg e-commerce-enabled sites, or they may offer information or additional features that set them aside from other vendors' sites of their type. Most straightforward commercial sites, which use the Internet solely as a promotional medium (and are described in Chapter 3 as 'corporate brochure' sites), have **not** been included in this book. For example, we have made no attempt to include a complete listing of the Web sites of, say, firms who repair computers. One reason for this is that if you live in Ashford, it will not help you to have to 'wade' through sites of firms in Barnsley. Another is that there are good sites *on the Internet* that do exactly this. You may have heard of Yahoo! or Yellow Pages, but have you heard of Scoot? (See Business essentials, page 78).

Wherever possible we have tried to find sites that help you find the commercial products and services you are looking for. 'Corporate brochure' sites perform a valuable function (if you are sure you want information about that company and they provide it). What the Internet does really well is to deliver up-to-the-minute information from the databases that lie behind the Web sites. We have included directories of vendors that are comprehensive, easily searchable and maintained on a daily or weekly basis. We have excluded those 'directories' where firms included have to pay, those that are patchy in coverage, are not maintained, or are impossibly difficult to use.

3

Web site types – a user's guide

We have all learnt to recognize types of television programmes, for example what a documentary looks like as opposed to a soap opera, or what to expect from the *Nine O'clock News*, but it is not quite so easy with Web sites. The Internet is a new medium and Web sites often cross over several forms and styles, borrowing from newspapers, advertising and television amongst many others. What's more, they are changing all the time.

However, there *are* recognizable characteristics that can help you identity what you can expect from a Web site. Getting familiar with these signs can help you pinpoint what type of Web page you've just stumbled on to and help you establish quickly whether it is going to be of any use to you. Read on for an introduction to the fascinating art of Web site spotting.

Seven types of Web site

Type one: the 'corporate brochure'

This type of site reflects the spectacularly boring efforts of a company that has usually just taken the text and images from its corporate brochure and put them online.

You will often find that these sorts of sites were constructed in a fit of enthusiasm; usually by firms who had just discovered the Web, and who thought they should have a Web presence. They had no clue about why or what they should do with it. In most cases, they simply transferred their promotional literature on to their Web site; now they wonder why no one ever visits it. As a consequence of this failure, and the subsequent loss of initial enthusiasm, these sites can fall into a state of chronic disrepair with little updating or maintenance. Others are updated but remain tedious.

You can recognize these sites by the fact they look like corporate brochures – typically the home page will feature glossy photographs or logos, and it is always the same thing on the 'menu': pages on Services (sales pitch) About Us (historically slanted sales pitch) and Products (relentless, full-frontal sales pitch). You won't find e-commerce on a corporate brochure site, nor any interactive features. You may be lucky and find an e-mail address, but don't be surprised if you don't get a reply when you use it.

You won't find any examples of corporate brochures in the guide as they don't satisfy our criteria for what makes a site useful. But you will find directory sites with links to many of these sites. If you want specific information about a particular company, then 'corporate brochure' sites can be useful.

Type 2: the 'labour of love'

The amateurish layout, the background that makes it harder to read the text, even the use of standard clipart, are all characteristics of a 'labour of love' Web site; usually created by an individual who is an obsessive enthusiast who wants to share his or her passion or knowledge about a subject with the rest of the world. These individuals collect links to absolutely everything they can find on the Internet, and sometimes add their own comments to the lists of links.

Whilst most 'labours of love' are the work of hobbyists, you will come across business-oriented Internet sites that are 'labours of love' and they *can* be very useful and informative. You need to exercise your discretion and decide for yourself. Often, like many works of art, 'labours of love' are left unfinished or are even abandoned, so don't presume the material presented is up to date or even accurate.

The following site, which deals with cryptography, is an example of a 'labour of love' that is genuinely useful to e-commerce specialists with a deep interest in security matters.

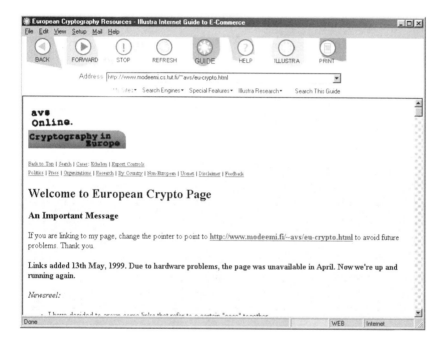

Type three: the 'flashy Flash'

The supreme example of the triumph of style over content, 'flashy Flash' sites tend to be hosted or created by designers or new media consultancies who want to show off their use of new media technologies (especially Macromedia's Flash animation package). Look out for intricate graphics, fancy dissolves and all things animated. The giveaway of a 'flashy Flash' site is a home page with something running across the screen for no obvious reason.

'Flashy Flash' sites can be bandwidth-hungry and tediously slow to download if you are working on a slow connection via a dial-up modem, or during peak-use times. The best of these sites should give you the option to switch off the animation and some will require plug-ins (such as Shockwave) before you can even get into them.

We've no examples of this type in the guide. They didn't meet our criteria because the technology intrudes so much that the content is pushed aside (or not there in the first place). But there *is* Flash animation on some of the sites in the guide; used properly it can make informative sites interesting and even entertaining.

Type four: the news site or 'cluttered portal'

The news format is becoming increasingly popular on the Internet since it uses conventions of magazine and newspaper publishing to make Web sites attractive and familiar to users. On the left-hand side of the news site Web page there is typically a navigation menu, in the centre is regularly changed news copy, and on the right is a list of sponsors or links to other editions or publications. Using the news format prompts readers to recognize the site as a publication with changing text, and will therefore encourages them to revisit it in the same way an individual might subscribe to a newspaper or magazine. They are often produced by offline publishers (such as the *Financial Times*) and focus on a specific interest area (as ZDnet does) or audience (as a trade journal would).

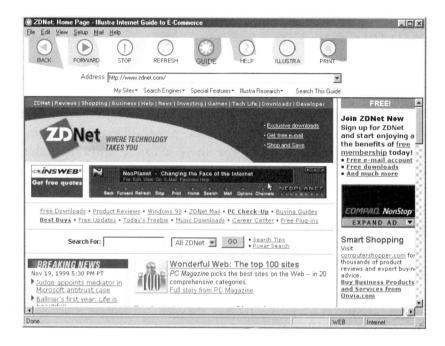

News sites can be well designed and pleasant to use. However, over-excitable site designers can try to stick too many menu options or links on their news sites – hence the 'cluttered portal' phenomenon, a serious trial for the eyes. This problem is further magnified when 8 pt type has been used by the Web designers in a effort to squeeze as much text into as small a space as possible.

News sites tend to be most useful if you want to browse in a particular subject area, rather than when you have a particular query or piece of information to look up. However, some people don't like browsing Internet sites and prefer to use paper publications so it is really down to you to try out news sites for yourself.

Type five: the 'cunningly concealed commercial'

Like promotional features in magazines that ape the editorial layout of their 'host', these Web sites are trying to sell you something but pretending that it is not their main purpose. Common examples include Web sites presented as 'information resources' or 'directories', but either you have to pay to use them, the entries in the 'directory' are actually paid adverts, or the 'resources' are trying to selling you the services of a consultant.

A quick way to spot the 'cunningly concealed commercial' is to go to the About Us section on the home page and find out who has created and maintains the site. You shouldn't necessarily reject this sort of site but we all like to know where we stand. We have rejected them for The Top 200 series, but we have included some commercial sites that offer genuinely useful information *in addition to* a sales pitch.

Type six: the 'dull but worthy'

Mostly produced by public bodies, such as a trade association or your local council, these sites usually provide useful information but often give little thought to making this a pleasurable or even straightforward process for their victim (the user).

Whilst the best can be accessible and sensibly organized, the worst will tell you what they do via a clunky and badly designed interface. Even more deadly is the tendency of some public body sites to feature numerous very boring documents on obscure aspects of regulatory or legislative procedure, presented as pages and pages of dense text. The more advanced of these will allow you to download their documents, sometimes in PDF format, for which you need the (free) Adobe Acrobat reader installed.

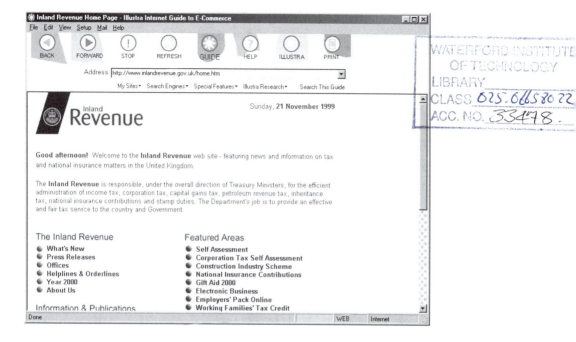

However, public Web sites are often useful as a first port of call when you need to deal with a particular agency, such as the highly recommended Inland Revenue site featured above, but public organizations often lack the resources and/or imagination to develop truly innovative sites.

Type seven: the 'firm favourite'

These Web sites are sheer pleasure to use. They come in all shapes and sizes, but they are the ones you return to again and again. 'Firm favourites' usually exploit the interactive potential of the Web to the full. They are innovative, imaginative and offer something that really meets the needs of Internet users. On them you will find searchable databases, delivered via well-designed and intuitive interfaces. They provide access to features, services and information that cannot easily be found elsewhere *on* or even *off* the Web. It is this combination of excellent, fully interactive design *and* high quality, genuinely useful information that makes a 'firm favourite' Web site.

Interestingly, it isn't just big players who can create these top-quality Web sites. In fact, it is often the simpler, more modest sites that exploit a clever idea with most flair and imagination. One example of this is found on the Multimap site. Here the linking of postcodes to online mapping makes it possible to provide a really useful service to anyone wanting to give directions to a particular place.

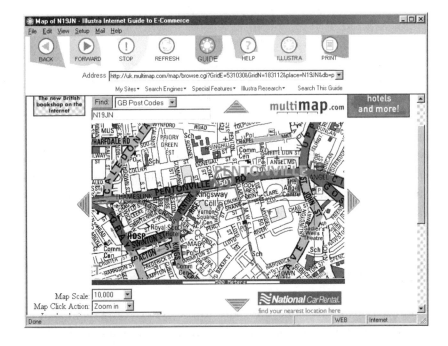

Sadly, 'firm favourites' are a rare occurrence on the Web. We can only hope that as site developers become more clued up, 'firm favourites' will become more common than the welcome exception they currently are. You will find such sites strongly featured in Business essentials.

4

Beyond the Web: e-mail and newsgroups

The hype around the Internet usually focuses upon the wonders of the World Wide Web, wowing us with 'cool' Web sites, the lure of e-commerce and the promised link-up with digital TV. But there are other tools available through the Net and it is worth considering their potential value before dashing off to surf those flashy sites.

E-mail is easy

With the spotlight on 'dot.com' companies these days, e-mail seems very much the poor relation of the Internet. Yet electronic mail is a fantastically flexible tool for business people. It is cheap to use, easy to understand and has a lot of hidden abilities. Having been around for 30 years (since the birth of the Net) it is not subject to some of the technical changes that might force you to update your Web browser every three months.

For many people e-mail is the best reason for being on the Internet. It is a cheap, convenient means of communicating, whether across the office or around the globe. It can be used to keep in touch with people who are asleep when you're awake, to share news and information with hundreds of people at the same time, and it can offer access to customers, specialist information and new markets.

It can improve productivity, promote discussion amongst dispersed teams, notify you of an order or let a customer know that you've got a sale on. It is rapidly becoming an essential tool of modern business and sits neatly alongside the phone, letters and face-to-face meetings as part of the way to get things done.

Are you getting the most from your e-mail?

Whatever you think of the Internet, it is becoming increasingly difficult to avoid the use of e-mail. Anyone who can use a word processor can compose a message and send it to one, twenty or ten thousand people at the press of a button.

Despite fears about the growth of viruses and junk mail, the volume of e-mail traffic is expanding even faster than the general growth of the Net. With the growing convergence of e-mail with mobile phones and faxes, that level of expansion can only increase.

One-to-one e-mail

The starting point for e-mail is usually to see it as a substitute for an answerphone. I send you a message, which you receive when you check your mailbox. You compose a reply and send it back, so that I can pick it up when I next check my mail. It is an *asynchronous* means of communicating that has many benefits over the spoken word.

For a start, most people tend not to write in the same way as they speak. We tend to use whole sentences, for example, comprising complete words, and consider our message more carefully and for longer before committing it to paper, so a written message can often be clearer and more logically constructed than a spoken one. This helps both parties enormously. Replies can be more considered when you don't have to think instantly as you do on the telephone.

If I write you an e-mail you can include my words in your reply. There is no need to spend ages explaining exactly what you're replying to, when you can copy my question back to me followed by a simple 'yes' or 'no'. You may want to copy my e-mail message into a word-processing document, or make some other use of it, without having to type anything yourself. You can forward it to someone else at a stroke, or copy others in on an exchange with a mutual colleague.

Of course a quick telephone call can be far more productive than a series of disjointed e-mails, and a chat over a pint is usually far more conducive to reaching an agreement than struggling to type with one finger. But as an option for one-to-one communication it offers advantages over phone, faxes and meetings that should not be underestimated.

One-to-many e-mail

The penetration of e-mail amongst the general population has created a huge impetus for sending e-mail to lots of people in one go. The cost advantages over traditional mailing options are over-whelming, and the economy of scale is mind-blowing. Why send one message to one person by post for 20p when for about 5p (the current BT minimum charge) you can go online and send an e-mail to hundreds of people and for 10p send it to thousands.

Spam

The Internet community has long known of the potential benefits of mass mailing and has recognized that it also the potential to drown the Internet in a tide of e-mail. Because it is so difficult to regulate anything online, it has been left to Internet users them-selves to seek to control the use of 'spam' – the name coined for the use of unsolicited e-mail sent to hundreds or thousands of people at the same time, usually through a mailing list or newsgroup that somebody else has created. It should be distinguished from targeted e-mail sent to a mailing list that you or your company have created.

If you need to know more about a term like 'spam' – and whether it did indeed originate from that Monty Python sketch – you can make use of the Writing aids section in Business essentials. The invaluable *Webopedia* also helps you out:

Many direct-marketing professionals view e-mail as manna from heaven, and list brokers have traded in e-mail addresses for many years. As with a lot of tactics such as these, most people only use them because they are successful, and there are plenty of Web sites that explain how they work, and how to integrate e-mail mailings with other marketing tools. You need to know about them, both because you will receive them and because you may want to send them as part of your business.

Is free e-mail worth it?

The number of people with e-mail has escalated sharply in the past year or so, thanks to the number using free e-mail services such as Hotmail. These are usually accessed through a Web page and make it possible to get and send messages anywhere that you can log on to the Net. The phenomenal growth of cybercafés in such traveller-friendly destinations as Thailand and Australia is testament to how convenient such services can be when you're on the move.

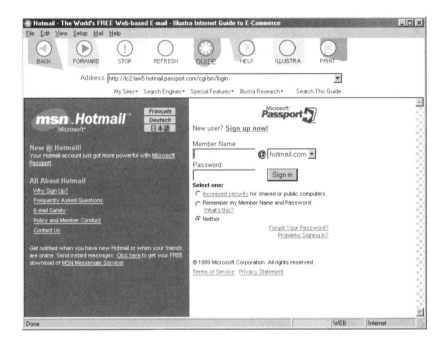

While free systems are great for personal use, most business people will be looking for something slightly different, both in terms of security and the desire to link e-mail in with their overall online presence. There is little credibility in using a Hotmail account for business, compared to owning a domain name (eg www.yourbusinessname.co.uk) and having an e-mail address to go with it.

Many-to-many e-mail

This type of e-mail communication is becoming recognized by many in the Net-literate business community as an important part of building lasting relationships with customers. You can send customized e-mails to your customers and they can e-mail you and each other to take part in online discussions. You can use a free service (such as eGroups) or you could buy software to build this capability into your Web site.

Newsgroups

Newsgroups are considered a nether region of the Internet, not usually travelled by the average Internet punter and populated by mythological Internet gurus who swap hackers' codes, dirty pictures and inane gossip. This is all true, but there is more to it than that.

Somewhere in your e-mail package or Web browser you'll have 'stumbled across' something to do with newsgroups, or read about them in magazines or an Internet guidebook. It is very easy to ignore them as it requires a bit of work to get the best out of them, but you may find pearls of wisdom, new contacts or the answer to a technical question, which makes it all worthwhile.

This is not news

The first point is that newsgroups are not full of news. They are electronic forums that discuss specific topics, identified by a name such as uk.jobs.wanted, alt.biz.misc, or even alt.recovery.cow-fetish. Anyone can post a message to a forum, and everyone subscribed to it will receive it. Everyone else in the group can then see any reply to the message.

At its simplest a newsgroup is a straightforward discussion tool, enabling people with similar interests to ask questions, share information and swap gossip. There may be a group relating to the trade you're in, a country you're interested in exporting to, or a piece of software you're having problems with. It may be a useful source of advice, a way of raising your profile in a niche market or somewhere to check out your ideas before presenting them to your boss.

There are some 25,000 of those groups out there, running through a piece of technology called Usenet. The whole thing is e-mail based, and to join the discussion you need to be subscribed to a group. Netscape's and Microsoft's browser packages include software for reading newsgroups, but it does take a bit of setting up for the beginner.

Another route into the world of newsgroups is the amazing www.deja.com. This site catalogues the messages on nearly every newsgroup and has archives going back to 1995 on some lists. It has a search facility to help track down useful groups, and lots of other add-ons to link you into related stuff. It has recently become more of a portal to consumers, but you can still find what you want from the newsgroups if you 'dig deep'.

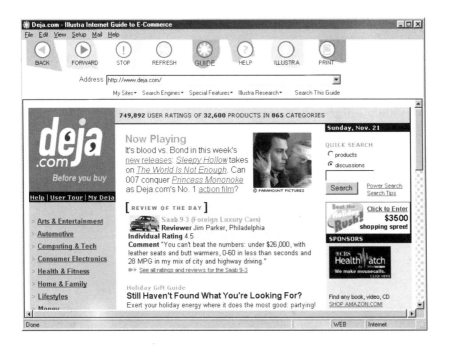

Using newsgroups

Newsgroups are not for everyone. They can seem difficult to use and often appear to be inhabited by people who are either too knowledgeable or simply too intimidating to deal with. But they could be a great source of help and many people swear by them for up-to-the-minute interaction with others anywhere in the world.

Specialist newsreader software is available to help make reading easy and you can download messages when you check your e-mail. They can be delivered amongst your regular e-mail, or browsed online. You can keep tabs on any number of lists by using the software to subscribe to them, and either check them as they come in or leave half an hour aside now and then to read back through recent messages.

To find the best list for you, start at www.deja.com and begin searching for subjects. Many newsgroups relate to recreational activity, so serious business information can be hard to come by at first. Have a good 'rummage around' the site, though, use the search facilities, think laterally, join lists you like the look of, and you'll soon get the hang of it.

Newsgroups are not the most user-friendly of technologies and there's no point spending frustrated hours trying to make them work for you. But they're obviously only there because they work for millions of people, and it's just possible that could include you.

5

Small businesses and the Internet

What are Web sites for small businesses like?

The first vitally important point to digest is **useful small-business Web sites are** *not* like useful small-business books. Web sites that are useful for small businesses will not be necessary labelled as 'small business' sites. Web pages that you, as a business user, will find relevant are hosted by a myriad of different organizations, companies and individuals, all with different agendas and very different interests. This may sound confusing, but this diversity is one of the *key* strengths of using the Web as a source of information.

We are used to small business as a subject topic, which in book publishing generally covers a predictable and defined area of information provision. We know what topics will be covered – book keeping, business strategy and marketing amongst many others. What's more, small-business books sit in a certain shelf in the bookshop making them easy to locate and identify.

Information on the Web fulfils more than one business function

Material relevant to small businesses available on the Internet is much less clearly defined than in book publishing, and it can be difficult to recognize which Web sites are aimed at business audiences. Moreover, some sites that aren't labelled 'small business' will still be useful to the business user. This is further complicated by the fact that users also have to work out which sites are any good for what they want to find out. It is not surprising that so many people find using the Internet a confusing and complicated process.

Nevertheless, the Web *is* a good information tool for small businesses because it provides a diverse range of information functions that business-oriented books or newspapers cannot easily compete with. For example, you can and probably will use the Internet for checking train times, finding the cheapest office supplies, researching competition, networking on a global scale, browsing news sites, downloading forms, studying online business resources, comparing flight prices and even for light relief when the strain of the office gets too much for you.

To help you get to grips with the ways in which small businesses can, and do, make use of Web sites, we've compiled the following small-business Web site checklist.

Small-Business Web Site Checklist

When you encounter an unfamiliar Web site, which of the following types does it most resemble?

Directories

These allow you to locate specific information via a searchable database. Directories can be general such as the online Yellow Pages or specific such as the database on the Companies House Web site.

Corporate brochures

These are often visually imaginative, but lack interactive features (see Chapter 3 for more information about this type of site). They can be useful for doing background research on a particular company or organization.

Resources

These will provide information on a particular subject area and are usually described as 'resources' on the menu bar of the Web site. You also might come across them as dedicated small-business resource sites. Resources can appear as stand-alone Web pages, downloadable documents or extracts from books. Beware of individuals abusing the term 'resource'. They want to attract visitors with the allure of providing information but they are actually promoting products or services via a 'cunningly (or not so cunningly) concealed commercial'.

Online vendors

These allow purchasing, usually offering the possibility of transacting via the Internet by inputting credit card details.

Reference aids

You will go back to these again and again, to look up everything from train times, postcodes or words in online dictionaries. Reference aid sites are mostly included in Business essentials.

News sites

These contain information on general business matters or have specialist information, and the content is changed regularly (as in newspapers). Use them for general news browsing or for keeping up to date with new developments in a particular field.

What is this checklist for?

This small-business Web site checklist has been used in conjunction with the evaluation criteria described in Chapter 1 in order to select Web sites for inclusion in *The Top 200 Web Sites for Small Business*. It has been used to help determine the relevance score you'll find next to each Web site review.

There are countless Web sites that don't offer British business users the possibilities we've outlined in the checklist. It could be because they are aimed at a different audience, or they may be poorly designed efforts that are merely trying to sell you something. Neither of these sorts of sites appear in this guide. But the Internet taken as a whole is an immensely useful resource. See Chapter 9 for some guidance about conducting your own small-business research.

But what about sites that actually are labelled as small-business sites? They do exist, but at this point in the history of the Internet they tend to be US based. It is often banks or financial institutions, who seek small businesses as their customers, who provide them; for example, American Express Small Business Exchange. As well as supplying useful information, these sites feature a soft-sell for the provider's services.

Other general sites seek to become 'portals', or entry points to the Web, for small-business users, and try to make revenue from advertising or links to sites providing commercial services. Netscape, now part of America Online, developed its Netcenter as part of a portal strategy.

Since the United States is more advanced in Internet adoption than the United Kingdom, it is not surprising that a larger number of small-business Web sites are located across the Atlantic.

This leads us on to the second important point: most Web sites are US based. This is inevitably going to change as the Internet becomes more widely used in the UK and the rest of the world, but at the moment the vast majority of business-oriented Web sites are designed for US audiences. For the British business user some of the material is still useful but the more culturally specific content is not. The US Web sites in the Top 200 have been included because they are relevant to British business users. However, when you venture beyond this guide you will have to be prepared for the US slant, which will characterize much of the material you come across.

6

Getting basic information

For ease of use, we've divided the Top 200 small-business sites into 11 topic areas. You'll find a full list of these sites at the end of the book, but for fast access install the CD ROM on your computer and access them via your desktop. If you do this it will also allow you to click directly on to the Web sites reviewed instead of having to type Web site addresses into your Internet browser.

The following chapters give you an overview of what kind of material you are likely to find in each topic, as well as what sorts of Web sites you can expect to find in a particular subject area. Remember, this will be constantly changing, so make sure you update your guide regularly, which you can do by visiting the Illustra Web site. After you have installed the CD ROM you can do this directly by clicking the Illustra button.

General sites

These sites aim to collect a lot of useful information into one place, and can be useful stepping-off points to explore subjects in more detail by following links on their pages. The UK Business Net, for example, is aiming to build a series of useful directories and resource centres, including one where you can send your press releases. It also collects links and aims to be a guide to the Internet for business. There is no advertising on the site, but apart from the companies database where entries are free, you have to pay to be included. You should bear this in mind when considering how comprehensive the information is. One problem with this site is that it is impossible to find out who runs it; only the company name UK Business Net Ltd is given, which is not even featured in the site's companies database. However, the links can be helpful and the diary of forthcoming events is good.

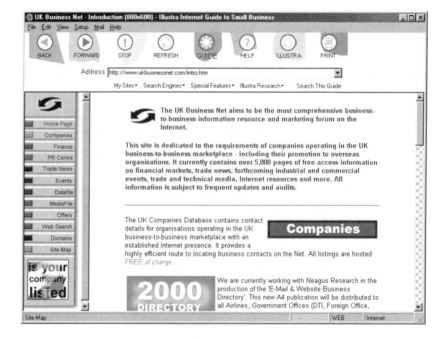

We have looked at, and rejected, a number of sites that aim to provide useful general information for small businesses. There is nothing in the UK yet to match the best of the US sites, and we have included these because they still offer more to UK small businesses than the homegrown ones.

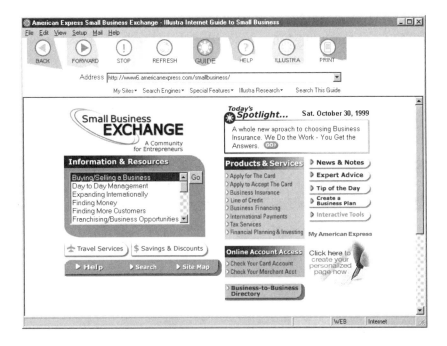

American Express are of course trying to sell you their financial services, but at the same time they offer useful advice. The site's sections on marketing and management are more relevant to UK users than those on law and finance.

The Department of Trade and Industry's Web site (see General – National bodies) offers some good advice itself, and links to other Web sites, such as the Business Link National Site. The situation may improve when the new Small Business Service, loosely modelled on the US government's Small Business Administration and announced in the Budget speech in March 1999, is implemented. The DTI's Information Society Initiative (see Technology – Development support) has many resources for small firms including case studies of good practice in the use of new technologies. Other UK general small-business sites are disappointing, but there are several initiatives in the pipeline. We will be monitoring these, so be sure to click the Illustra button on your guide to keep it up to date.

The Federation of Small Businesses ought to be a good place to start – this is one of the 'dull but worthy' sites described in Chapter 3.

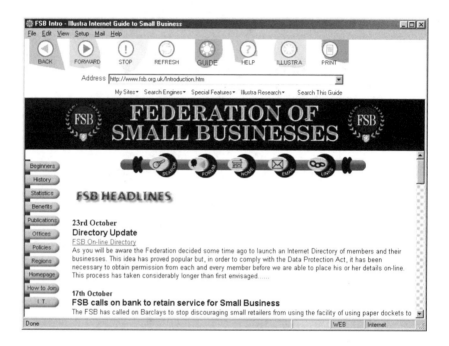

The site has a good section marked 'Beginners' for those new to the Internet, rather than for business. Other than this, the site tells you about the FSB and its activities, rather than offering information that would make you want to have this as one of your 'firm favourites'. Really good Web sites are designed for the user, not for the organization. If you enter a department store, you want signs to the various departments, not a list of directors and an organizational diagram. As the Internet develops we hope that all kinds of organizations will understand this point.

7

Managing your business

Finance

Key points

The Internet offers:

- up-to-date financial reference sources and news;
- searchable databases on financial subjects, eg insolvency and investment;
- online credit management and financial services, including banking.

The US bias makes many business-oriented finance sites irrelevant to the UK audience, since financial regulations or resources do not pop pop easily across different national economies. However, the Web is good for general browsing for financial information, eg at **ft.com**, or in particular subject areas, eg the **Chartered Institute of Taxation**.

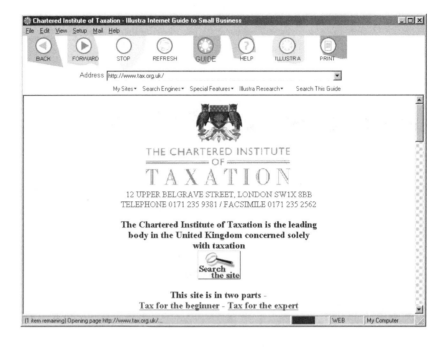

Types of financial Web sites

Financial sites for small-business users tend to fall into three categories:

- News sites with coverage of financial affairs. These are good for general browsing, and content is changed on a daily basis. The *Financial Times'* Web site allows you to see back articles free for a month, after which you have to pay a small fee for using its archive.

- Government or official bodies' Web sites, eg **The British Venture Capital Association** or the **Inland Revenue**. These will be of use when looking for specific information and, even if you want information that isn't on their Web site, you can e-mail the organization with your request for further information. The **Insolvency Service** has an invaluable guide to insolvency law and practice, which it would be better to read *before* the creditors are knocking at the door.

- Financial vendors' sites (eg tax consultants', banks' sites). These vary enormously in quality and sophistication but are, nevertheless, all 'cunningly concealed commercials.' Rather than list these sites, we have tried to find those which are themselves lists or directories, eg **AAAdir** which maintains the most comprehensive list of banks we have found.

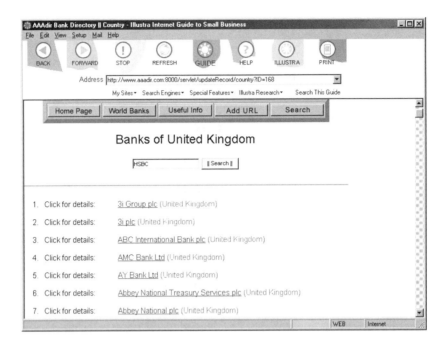

This does not mean you should always dismiss vendors' sites altogether; for instance the **Kestrel Taxation Services** Web site may be a crudely designed 'labour of love' from a tax consultant, but it does contain some handy insights as well. Likewise the **Banking Liaison Group**, run by former bank managers, won't win any design or usability prizes, but there are 'nuggets' if you 'dig' for them.

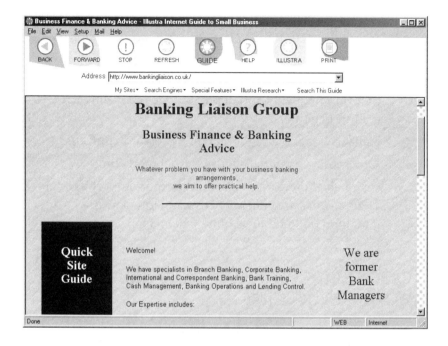

Sales and marketing

Key points

On the Internet you can find:

- pointers on how to develop a marketing strategy;
- searchable databases for identifying sales opportunities;
- extensive data available for market research purposes, although not all of it is free.

The Internet is full of sales material delivered by over-excitable marketing people, but you have to look long and hard to find genuinely useful resources on sales and marketing. It *is* there, although much of the information can be quite basic. The following represent the different types of marketing information you are likely to encounter:

▨ Online magazines and news aimed at marketing professionals but also of potential interest to small-business users.

▨ Marketing resources often produced by large corporations that vary in quality and depth, but are often aimed at relative beginners.

▨ Statistical data to use for marketing research purposes.

▨ A plethora of material about Internet marketing.

▨ Searchable directories for locating export/import partners. The free ones are generally government-sponsored initiatives but tend to be quite patchy in coverage.

CASE STUDY:
Writing a marketing plan

You run an entertainments and events management business, virtually single-handedly. It has worked fairly successfully on a small scale for the past two years with business being generated mainly by word of mouth recommendation. However, now you want to expand and formalize what you do. Devising a proper marketing plan is one of the key methods by which you hope to do this. How can the Internet help?

All the sites listed under General in Sales and Marketing will be of use to you. Start with the **Marketing UK** Web site, which has two excellent sections, Marketing Planning and Marketing Healthcheck, both of which will prompt you to start asking the right questions.

Visit the **Center for Business Planning Resources** for an excellent article on how to devise a marketing plan and for examples of good practice that will help you compile your dream document.

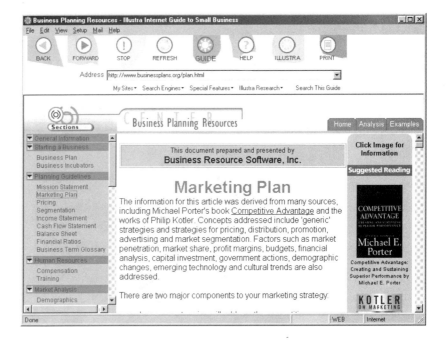

Personnel and training

Key points

- High-quality training and personnel management resources are available online, usually from US-based training agencies.

- The Web is 'riddled' with training consultants trying to sell their services.

- The Internet is a good tool for recruitment and/or job hunting which (unlike national newspapers) has a global reach.

Once the 'cunningly (or not so cunningly) concealed commercials' have been discarded, there are a number of useful resources on the Web for business users interested in personnel management and training. You can spot the sales-pitch-only sites by looking for a resource button in the main menu. If the 'resources' reveal information about how wonderful a particular consultant is or a 'fabulous offer' to purchase a book, then you can beat a hasty retreat.

CASE STUDY:
How to create training events

You are the general manager of an electronics store. Your boss has asked you to devise some training to improve the shop-workers' time management skills. You have done this before informally several times, but now she wants a formal written outline of what you are going to do, which needs to be on her desk by Monday. What do you do?

You go to **Training Zone's Toolkit** Web site to see what resources are available on time management, and you download a useful piece called 'Techniques for getting organised' that you can use as a handout for the training (see Personnel and training – Personal development).

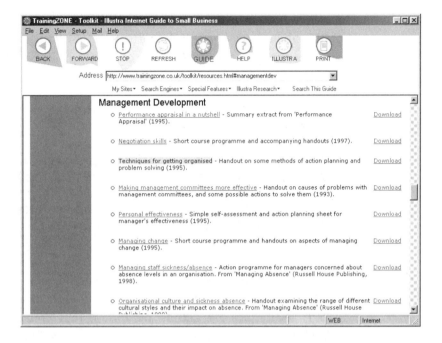

In the same section of the guide you find a time management quiz on the **American Express** site that you will also use for training purposes.

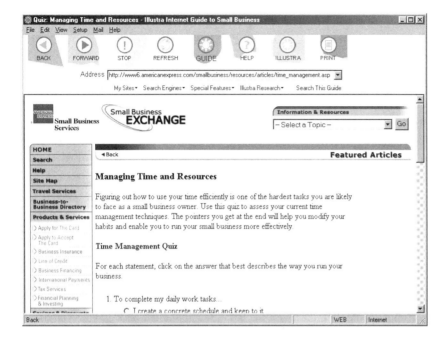

You go to a piece called 'Training Needs Analysis' from the same toolkit on the **Training Zone** Web site and find that it offers an excellent model of how to set out a training event outline. You use it as a model for the outline you hand to your boss. The outline is handed to your boss with some Dilbert cartoons (from **Catbert's Anti-Career Zone**) pasted in as illustrations for light relief and to put your boss in a good mood.

Purchasing

Key points

- E-commerce has enabled online office purchasing.
- There is a wide variation in site quality, site design and delivery pricing.
- Some vendors operate wholly online.

░ You can perform extensive searches for niche consumer products that might be difficult to track down in your locality.

The Internet has a capacity to store large amounts of data that can be easily searched and nicely illustrated. This makes it a great vehicle for the office supply catalogue and saves phoning or faxing orders. You can also browse without incurring a sales pitch and leave the 'shop' at a click of the mouse. As well as office supply sites, we've included some general shopping sites in this section to give you an idea of what else is out there and for enlivening your lunch breaks.

CASE STUDY:
How to purchase office supplies online

You are the office administrator for a small company and want to try out office supply purchasing online for the first time. You're fed up with your current supplier and think using the Internet might save time and allow you to shop around for bargains, but you have a lot of misgivings about it. What will it involve and how complicated will it be?

Firstly, go to a reputable vendor, perhaps one you have dealt with offline or who has been recommended to you. The best sites will offer purchasing via a secure Internet connection (where your financial details are safely encrypted) and a very simple and straight-forward interface that even the most nervous novice will find easy to use. Good sites will also give you the option to phone in with credit card details if you're feeling very cautious about buying online. Checking whether office supply sites offer these facilities will help you judge how user friendly the vendor is, and whether they are worthy of your custom.

Browse a number of sites to give you an idea of what is available before you order and check delivery costs, which vary hugely. Start with the **Viking Direct** and **Office Shopper** sites. **Viking direct** is an excellent site, well illustrated with an ordering system that is efficient and easy to use. Look at the 'security statement' at the bottom of the left hand menu/frame for information that might help to combat your misgivings about online shopping. (See Supplies and purchasing – Office supplies, or type in Viking in Search This Guide.)

In the same section of the guide, the **Office Shopper** site has an attractive design and is also wonderfully easy to use.

Travel

Key points

- Search facilities allow easy comparison of fares and make the Web good for bargain hunting.

▓ Sites offer a wealth of up-to-date information useful for travellers including checking flights delays at UK airports, weather forecasts and currency conversion.

▓ Transaction services available include online hotel and flight booking, and car hire.

Travel sites listed in the guide are not directed exclusively to business travellers: those travelling on business or pleasure will find them useful.

The most commonly used facilities on these sites include searching for flights, accommodation or last-minute package deals. They are great fun to use but bear in mind that, like travel agents' adverts, many of the featured 'bargains' evaporate when you start checking availability. You can book online but many users prefer to use these sites for 'window shopping' and then contact airlines or hotels directly to book.

Also useful is the Internet's capacity to give you access to timetables for a wide variety of transport systems. For example, check out the **Railtrack** timetable (see Business essentials) and the excellent **UK Public Transport Information** site.

CASE STUDY:
From Doncaster to Paris via the Internet

You are the technical director of an electronics firm based in Doncaster and you want to attend a trade fair in Paris next month. How can you use the Internet to cater for all your travel needs?

You've decided to go by train, so you access the **Eurostar** Web site to check departure times. You find a time that suits you and get your secretary to book you a 1.57 pm departure from Waterloo. You go to the interactive timetable on the **Railtrack** site to find out which train will get you into King's Cross from Doncaster in good time to get to Waterloo.

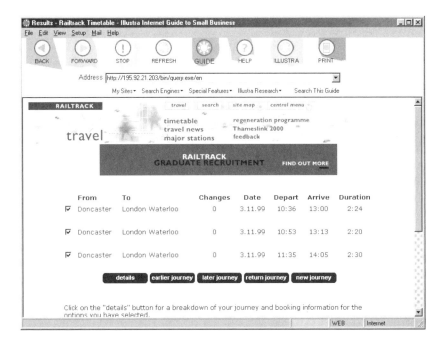

There are two trains listed, so you decide to take the earlier one in case there are leaves on the line.

Next, you look at the **Expedia UK** Web site and book a hotel in Paris. You go to the **Systran** site and pop pop the Web site of the German company who will also be at the trade show and who you are hoping to get some business from. This is a simple matter of typing in the company's Web address (or URL). Although you should not expect a perfect translation from a computer you should get an adequate version.

8

Finding more – doing business research

So far we've looked at how to use *The Top 200 Web Sites for Small Business* to see what's on the Net to help you with the basic business functions.

In this chapter we'll see how you can use the guide as a tool for research, either for relevant background information, eg on the legal context of small business, or on how to apply for a grant from the European Union or get further into relevant technology issues.

Legal context

Key points

▪ Many Web sites giving legal information are geared to legal professionals rather than business users.

▪ There is patchy coverage of legal information for businesses on the Internet although there are strengths in certain areas, eg insolvency.

▪ Such Web sites are useful to give you a quick overview before you seek legal advice.

The legal profession has a reputation for being old-fashioned and conservative and perhaps this is why many legal Web sites are not terribly imaginative or useful for business users. The usual offerings tend to be from legal firms with uninspiring 'corporate brochures' or from 'dull but worthy' governmental or public bodies that present legislation via drab and text heavy Web sites. There are some areas that receive better coverage and these are highlighted in the guide.

CASE STUDY:
Patent Law for beginners

Your company has invested heavily in R&D over the last few years, and now it has a product application that you would like to patent. You are new to this area and know nothing about the process, but you do know that patent lawyers cost a fortune and you would therefore like to do as much homework as possible before going to see one. Why use the Web?

The Web is no substitute for qualified professional advice but it can give you an excellent starting point. The best resources in this area are from national bodies. As a beginner you need go no further than the smart and highly accessible **Patent Office** Web site. This site has an excellent 'newcomer's guide' which will tell you everything you need to get started, and also features a searchable database of current patent applications held by the Patent Office.

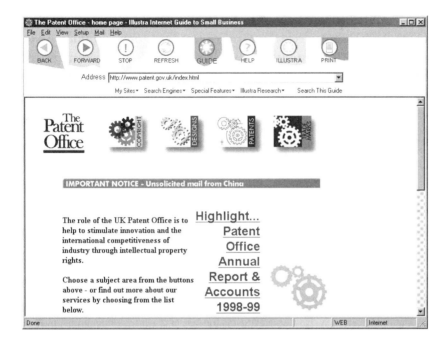

The Patent Office - home page - Illustra Internet Guide to Small Business

File Edit View Setup Mail Help

BACK FORWARD STOP REFRESH GUIDE HELP ILLUSTRA PRINT

Address http://www.patent.gov.uk/index.html

My Sites▾ Search Engines▾ Special Features▾ Illustra Research▾ Search This Guide

The
Patent
Office

COPYRIGHT DESIGNS PATENTS TRADE MARKS

IMPORTANT NOTICE - Unsolicited mail from China

The role of the UK Patent Office is to help to stimulate innovation and the international competitiveness of industry through intellectual property rights.

Choose a subject area from the buttons above - or find out more about our services by choosing from the list below.

Highlight...
Patent
Office
Annual
Report &
Accounts
1998-99

Done WEB Internet

Europe

Key Points

Web sites about Europe provide a good starting point for those researching EU business-funding programmes but are not very user-friendly. However, information about the euro available on the Web is extensive and helpful.

Europe is not a subject that has inspired many great online masterpieces, mainly because until fairly recently Internet activity has been concentrated in the US market. Most Europe-wide Internet information available to businesses is dire. However, if you need to do research on organizations such as the EU, the Web is an excellent starting point. You don't have to phone Brussels, you can get an overview of all EU programmes fairly quickly via the Internet and you can also make contact with a number of British-based agencies that aim to help steer businesses through the minefield of European business regulations and protocol.

What is currently absent on the Internet are resources that help British businesses maximize trading opportunities with Europe-based companies. Even though there are a number of Internet-based European directories that are attempting to do just that, they currently lack the scale and penetration to be as effective as they could be. As European economic and monetary union continues to develop apace this is likely to change, so European Web sites are ones to keep coming back to.

CASE STUDY:
Applying for European business funding

You are the MD of a chemical engineering company in Strathclyde, which intends to apply for business funding to aid the development of a new micro-processor control unit that your R&D unit is currently prototyping. You would like to consider European funding but are daunted by the jargon and bad press the whole process has been given by other firms in your area who have also attempted to do this. How could you use the Internet to further your ambitions?

Firstly, go to the **UK Business Incubation** Web site where you will find an invaluable glossary of funding terms. It would be helpful if there were a simple way of printing out the whole glossary, but there isn't. It is particularly useful for deciphering European funding acronyms, therefore it's worth opening another window (click File – New Window on the top of the guide) so you have it available when you plough through the other sites. More general information about business funding is also available on the rest of the site.

The Office of Science and Technology has a helpful 'Miniguide to the Fifth Framework Programme' written in plain English appearing in the Science and Technology section of the **Department of Trade and Industry's** main Web site.

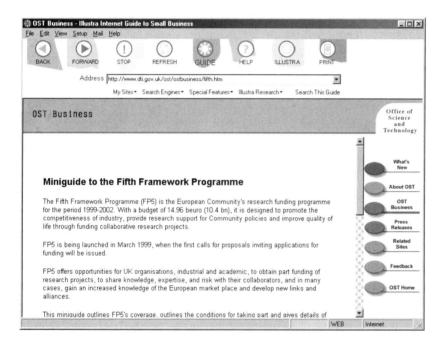

It is also worth looking at the Web site of the **UK Network of Euro Info Centres**, which might be able to provide you with useful contacts if you e-mail a request.

Technology

Key points

- The Internet offers access to large amounts of free and low-cost software which can be downloaded via Web sites.

- Up-to-date, high-quality, free information about technology developments (mostly in the computer and IT sector) is available.

- There are large numbers of resources that will improve your use of the Internet.

Whereas books date quickly and struggle to keep pace with fast-moving technology developments, Web sites are easy to update and feature huge amounts of information about IT. Even the most technophobic amongst you will find some resources useful, such as **Webopedia**, the reference guide to computer jargon. Technophiles, on the other hand, can 'wallow' in the vast array of technology news sites and resources that the Internet has to offer. The shareware sites are best visited if you are an enthusiast or you know what you are looking for. Unfortunately industrial technologies (such as CAD or CAM) are not as well represented on the Internet as IT in general, but you can use **AskMagpie** (in Business essentials – News and media) to check whether a trade journal exists for your industry.

CASE STUDY:
Looking for industry-specific technology information

You are the director of a plastics manufacturing company. You would like to use the Internet to get access to technology information relevant to your industry, but most of the technology news you have found online relates to Silicon Valley-style hi-tech companies and not for companies in the more traditional manufacturing sector in which you are based. What can you do?

The first thing to remember is that manufacturing technologies are not well represented on the Internet compared to the IT sector.

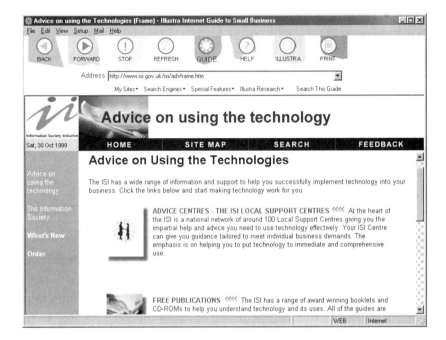

The Web site of the DTI's **Information Society Initiative** is aimed at all industrial sectors, but gives details about Local Support Centres and has downloadable documents on new technology written in plain English. In a section entitled 'Advice on using the technologies' it has examples of good practice, including a plastics manufacturing company (Plade). The **DTI** main Web site is also worth a look and you can do a search on their Web site to find relevant information on the plastics industry.

Go the directory section of the **Trade Association Forum** Web site (see General – Trade associations) to find out whether the British Plastics Federation has a Web site (it has).

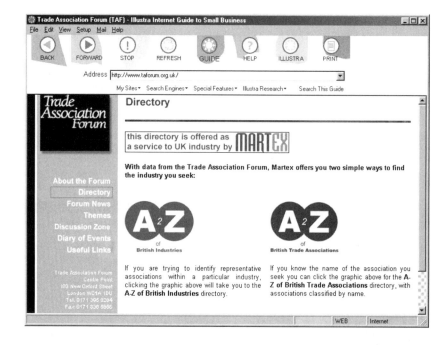

Use Chapter 4 of this book to help you access newsgroups and perform searches that can help you identify the very specific technology information you require.

E-commerce

Key Points

The Internet offers a huge range of information about e-commerce, ranging from guides aimed at the absolute beginner to sophisticated research papers. The vast majority of the material available originates from the United States.

The Web is the natural home of information about e-commerce, since it is able to keep up to date with the fast-moving market and technology changes that characterize this area. Furthermore, much of the focus of e-commerce centres on analysis of

Internet adoption and use patterns, making the Internet a logical place to look for such material. Any individual interested in finding out more about e-commerce should make the Web his or her first port of call.

In this subject area you will find infinite Web sites endlessly telling you who is online and what they are doing. Exercise due caution with many of these sites since they often originate from hard-nosed consultants who want to 'dazzle' you with statistics and 'whip up' excitement that will aid them in selling their services.

The US bias of most e-commerce Web sites means that UK businesses will need to think long and hard about what is useful and appropriate. Here we have concentrated on beginner-oriented material that gives business users in the UK a good starting point on the subject. For a more detailed exploration of this subject check out *The Top 200 Web Sites on E-commerce* in the same series as this book.

CASE STUDY:
How to sell guitars online

You run a business selling handmade guitars and you have a healthy mail order client list and generate respectable sales through local distributors. Now you would like to establish whether moving into e-commerce would benefit the company; you think it might help you move into different markets and enable you to compete with larger competitors. However, you are quite suspicious of doing research about the subject via Web sites that are trying to sell you their e-commerce products. Where would you start looking?

It is true that consultants, or companies with products or services to sell, host many of the e-commerce Web sites. However, on the good sites you will also be able to get high-quality advice as well.

The **Internet.Works** guide to e-commerce is an excellent starting point and will get you thinking about the important issues.

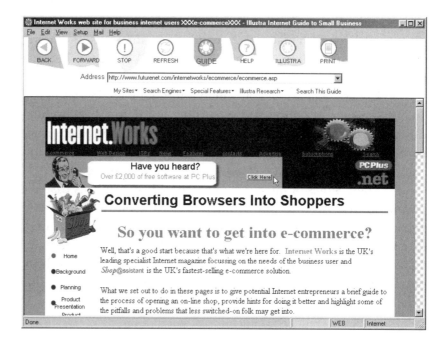

Sell it on the Web is also beginner-friendly and has useful features for newcomers to the subject including Frequently Asked Questions. The site also has a less busy and easier to navigate interface than some of the other e-commerce resource sites, which as 'cluttered portals' can be quite intimidating for beginners to a subject (see Chapter 3). Case studies are available on both of these sites and are valuable for beginners to look at, although virtually all you will come across are studies of US firms that may not pop pop comfortably across the Atlantic.

9

Getting out on your own

In this chapter we'll start with what's in the guide, and then give you some tips on how to search for material that's out there on the Internet. If you come across a site that you think should be included in the guide, then please let us know by clicking on My Sites, Add New Site and then Add and Recommend to Illustra Research. There's a reward for suggestions that meet our criteria for inclusion in our guides.

How to check out small business sites for yourself

So far, this book has concentrated on searching for business information in the guide. What about when you want to go out and explore the Web on your own? We've all experienced or heard the common complaints about searching the Web for information. Do any of these sound familiar?

It's too slow

I don't know where to start looking

When I use a search engine it throws up thousands of results and most of those are irrelevant

Most of what I come across is rubbish. . . there's no quality control

The results I get back aren't worth the effort, I've no time to use the Web.

Yes, the Internet *is* a sprawling jungle of information, and search engines are crude and inadequate tools. However, you can work to maximize your chances of successful searching by following certain rules. Read the following cautionary tale as an example of good use and ineffective use of the Internet.

CASE STUDY:
How to use and how not to use the Internet

Julie is a self-employed graphic designer who works on her own from a small office. She recently signed up for a free Internet account that she accesses from a dial-up connection via a modem and her office computer. She uses e-mail regularly and has dabbled on the Web. She would like to try using the Internet to get more work but doesn't really know where to start. What should she do?

The bad searcher

Julie sits down and types the words 'work' 'graphic design' and 'business' in varying combinations in a series of different search engines. She is slightly daunted by the thousands (in some cases millions) of Web sites that are turned up by her search requests, but she begins to plough dutifully through them. After the first 100 or so she is beginning to get impatient. Many results are different pages on the same Web sites and most are US-based graphic design companies advertising their services. What's more, as the afternoon progresses, the connection gets painfully slow and after 300 or so Web sites Julie gets fed up and goes to make a cup of tea, concluding that 'the Internet is a complete waste of time'.

The good searcher

Julie decides to start searching early the next morning when the connection is faster. In the meantime she sits down and thinks hard about what sort of information she is looking for from her Internet session. She concludes that what she really wants is to network with other firms and agencies in her local area who could offer her contract work. When she gets online she uses **AskAlex** (http:// www.askalex.co.uk) to search for graphic design companies in her area (Bristol).

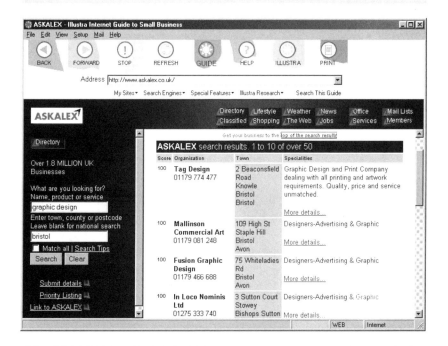

As a good searcher, Julie notices the small print above the search results, and learns that companies can pay to have their results appear at the top of the list. Bearing this in mind, she scrolls down and finds a number of possibilities.

She prints out copies of their Web sites for background research and e-mails copies of her CV to those that have an e-mail address. For the others she uses the post. She prints out the phone numbers and resolves to start doing follow-up phone calls next week.

She goes to the **Trade Association Forum** Web site and uses their directory to get to the Web site of the Design Business Association. She finds the link on the TAF site won't redirect her there so she uses Copernic (see the Search Engines feature) to search for 'design business association' and finds out why the link did not work.

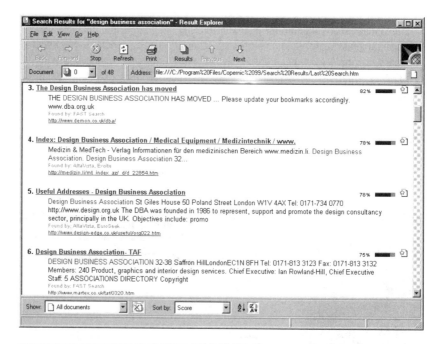

Julie finds a business link site that directs her to a free online recruitment service hosted by the Design Business Association. She browses through to see what sort of rates she can currently expect to charge and idly contemplates applying for a job in Portugal. Julie goes and makes a cup of tea, with a sense of having achieved something positive from her morning on the Internet.

How to maximize your search successes

You need to be prepared and focused on what you are looking for when you search the Web. Use the business Web site types checklist in Chapter 5 to help you focus on what sort of information you require. The frustration experienced by users who can't find the information they need is not only created by the low quality of information available on the Web, but also because they haven't clearly thought through what sort of information they want. The more focused you are in what types of sites you are looking for, the more successful you are likely to be.

Searching hints

- When you first reach a Web site check for a physical address and/or a date so that you can eliminate irrelevant US sites or those that are out of date or abandoned.
- Use meta search engines such as Copernic (which allow you to use several search engines at the same time by typing in the search terms only once). These give controlled results that are more reliable than those from any single search engines.
- Following links from useful sites can generate better results than blanket 'trawling' of search engines.
- Use the business checklist to establish which sort of sites you have found and whether they are going to useful.

And finally, here is a list of 'do's and don'ts', which summarize the key points to remember when you search the Internet for business information.

WWW searching for small-business sites – do's and don'ts

Do ...

Work out what type of information you want before you start.
Use Web sites types to help you decide what sites you have reached and what sites you are looking for. If the sites you have found don't tally with what you want to find then leave quickly.

Use search terms that are as specific as possible because they will get you better results.

Put 'UK business' in your search terms because it will help you

---

eliminate US sites which are less likely to be useful to British businesses.

Check the date of the last update when you find a site since this will save time-wasting on redundant or abandoned sites.

Don't ...

Feel that you should plough through all search results you return because this will inevitably waste time. Doing this is like reading every detail in a newspaper. Instead, make sure you read selectively.

Key in 'small business uk' as a search string and then wonder why you can't find the business information you want.

Search at peak times unless you want the Web to 'plod along' at a frustratingly slow pace. The best time to search is between 4 am and 7 am when the Web is wonderfully fast because the US market is asleep, not online.

Good Luck!!

The Top 200 Web sites for small business

Sub Topic	Title	Description		Rele-vance	Ease of Use
BUSINESS ESSENTIALS					
BUSINESS INFORMATION		The following sites contain financial, company and product information of value to any business user.			
	Interactive Investor International	Instant stock market quotes and access to some (occasionally) lively discussions from shareholders. Registration required.	www.iii.co.uk/	1	3
	Yahoo! Finance UK & Ireland	Simple instant stock market quotes without registration.	finance.uk. yahoo.com/	1	4
	CAROL	A set of over 3000 company reports from large companies in the UK, Asia and Europe. Registration is free to companies, but coverage can be patchy. You are transferred to the company's Web site, so reports are not in a standard format.	www.carol.co.uk/	1	2
	Companies House	Model Web site, beautifully designed. You can search the database for company information but (strangely) only on Monday to Friday from 8 am to 8 pm.	www.companies-house.gov.uk	2	3

Sub Topic	Title	Description		Rele-vance	Ease of Use
	How many online?	NUA Internet surveys collect data from around the world and give you the latest picture of how many people have Internet access in different countries.	www.nua.ie/surveys /how_many_online /index.html	1	2
	UpMyStreet	Enter your postcode and find out what your neighbourhood's really like. Gives data on house prices, crime clear-up rates, schools, council tax, and, if you're feeling fragile, ambulance response times. More features promised soon.	www.upmystreet.com/	2	4
	Scoot	One of the most useful and friendly sites around. Search by business type and area for anything you need. Free registration is needed to use the people finder which claims 17 million names on its database.	www.scoot.co.uk/	4	5
TRAVEL		Getting about is so much easier with this kind of constantly updated information at your fingertips. These sites provide a good excuse for spending money on a mobile Web terminal.			
	A2B Travel	A bit cluttered and not fully comprehensive, but this is the best general UK travel site we've encountered.	www.a2btravel.com/	3	2
	Expedia UK	Microsoft's UK travel site is an essential asset for the business traveller, but don't expect bargain travel here. It's simple to find scheduled flights, hotels and car hire in major cities and compare prices before you book.	expedia.co.uk/	3	4
	UK Public Transport Information	The site says 'If it's not here, it's not on the Web' and for once it's not hype. Everything you need to know about public transport in any part of the UK.	www.pti.org.uk/	4	4

Sub Topic	Title	Description		Rele-vance	Ease of Use
	Railtrack	If you simply want train times Railtrack's online timetable is the quickest way to get them.	195.92.21.203/bin/query.exe/en	4	3
	BAA Airport Information	Updates arrivals for major UK airports, and shows a flight timetable. You can also find out what's in the shops to buy while you're waiting for the flight.	www.baa.co.uk/	4	4
	World maps	Not just any old maps but just about every kind of map that might be out there. Some are detailed enough to see the street you're headed for, but most provide political, economic or geographical information that may be useful if you don't know a country well.	www.lib.utexas.edu/Libs/PCL/Map_collection/Map_collection.html	1	1
	OANDA Currency Converter	How many Albanian lek to the euro? No problem with this comprehensive and simple currency converter. You can also find historical rates for any day since 1990.	www.oanda.com/converter/classic	3	4
	Multimap.com	A clickable map, down to street level, of the whole UK. Or simply enter a place name, or postcode, and get a map which you can zoom in and out of. Terrific!	uk.multimap.com/map/places.cgi	4	5
WEATHER AND TIME		Time to find out whether you need an umbrella.			
	The Met. Office	The weather – 'straight from the horse's mouth'.	www.meto.govt.uk/	1	4
	The World Clock	Is it too late to call Melbourne? Instant time anywhere in the world.	www.timeanddate.com/worldclock/	2	1
TELEPHONE AND POST		Essentials about essentials.			
	Postcodes On-line	Find addresses from postcodes and vice versa.	www.royalmail.co.uk/paf/pcodefin.htm	4	4

Sub Topic	Title	Description		Rele-vance	Ease of Use
	UK Telephone code locator	In which part of the country is that number beginning 01736? (Penzance, actually). What's the code for Penrith? A simple and handy tool developed by an enthusiast.	www.warwick.ac.uk/ cgi-bin-Phones/nng	2	1
	BT PhoneNet UK	The UK phone book online. Even if you pay a dial-up call, it's cheaper than dialling 192.	www.bt.com/ phonenetuk/	4	4
	BT Friends and Family	Change your friends and family numbers at a stroke. You can also check the current status of your phone bill.	https://www.customer-service.bt.com/friends_family/owa/bestfriend.who	2	2
NEWS AND MEDIA		The best sites we've found for information about television, radio, newspapers and magazines			
	BBC News	The front page of the BBC's news Web site. You can link directly to the last news bulletin on the World Service or on BBC1, if your browser's equipped for sound and video.	news.bbc.co.uk/	2	4
	AskMagpie	Links to over 7000 magazines and often very specialist journals organized by subject in a well laid out front page. Sounds daunting, but a simple search engine allows title and subject searches. Many have Web links, but if not there are fax and phone numbers.	www.askmagpie.com/	3	4
	Media UK Internet Directory	A really comprehensive index to media resources. The use of sound quickly becomes irritating, but you'll need to turn it back up for the live TV and radio. Aims to please all, but would benefit by organizing the resources according to who the user is.	www.mediauk.com/ directory/	3	3
	World Newspapers Online	Lovely interface with clickable map to reach 120+ English language newspapers across the world.	www.alumni.adweb. co.uk/wno/	1	3

Sub Topic	Title	Description		Rele-vance	Ease of Use
	Teletext	Millions of people regularly use this service on their TV. On your computer it looks much better and is much easier to use.	www1.teletext.co.uk/	2	1
	TVPlus	Quick and simple guide to what is on the five terrestrial TV channels in your region plus a few satellite channels in peak-time only.	www1.teletext.co.uk/ tv_new/	1	1
WRITING AIDS		The online aids can be really useful for report writing – especially if you have a permanent connection to the Internet.			
	thesaurus.com	A simple online *Roget's Thesaurus*. You can put in UK spellings but will be given US spellings.	www.thesaurus.com/	1	2
	dictionary.com	Simple online dictionary based on Webster's.	www.dictionary.com/	1	2
	OneLook Dictionaries	If you're really stuck or a true word lover you'll get hooked on this database which claims to look at 2.8 million words in 566 dictionaries.	www.onelook.com/	1	2
	Webopedia	Look up what all that computer jargon means. If you really want to impress in 'techie' circles click on the recently added items and add them to your 'geekspeak'.	webopedia.internet .com/	2	3
	Whatis?com	Much more than a technical dictionary, this site has exploration sections on various topics, including how the Internet works, and speeds of connection. Try the learning paths section for excellent essay on technology-related topics such as 'convergence'.	www.whatis.com/	2	4
	infoplease.com	A huge US-based site with a huge number of … facts!	www.infoplease.com/	1	2

The Top 200 Web sites for small business

Sub Topic	Title	Description		Rele-vance	Ease of Use
	Microsoft Encarta	Microsoft's cut-down free online version of Encarta might find out what you need, if you can bear the hard sell for the subscription version.	www.encarta.msn.com	1	2
LAW AND MONEY		General resources – often enough to tell you whether you need to pay for professional advice.			
	adviceguide	A service from the Citizens Advice Bureau – well designed and easy to use.	www.adviceguide.org. uk/nacab/plsql/ nacab.homepage	1	3
	buy.co.uk	A simple but hugely effective idea. Put in your postcode and latest bill and you can see whether you'll save money by switching electricity or gas suppliers. Compares mobile phone tariffs as well.	www.buy.co.uk/	3	4
FOR ADVANCED USERS		These are free resources for those seriously into the Internet, or who work all day on a keyboard.			
	EBoz!	Links and tips for anyone involved in building or running a Web site, or who'd like to. Expert advice, case studies and discussion forums, and plenty of free downloads to get you going.	www.eboz.com/index. shtml	1	4
	AnyDay.com	If you use an electronic organizer or a program such as Microsoft Outlook you'll find this a terrific idea. You can store your information confidentially and free of charge on this site. You can synchronize it with your own data so that others (your secretary or work colleagues) can see your schedule if you share a password and login.	www.anyday.com/	2	4

Sub Topic	Title	Description		Rele-vance	Ease of Use
	Calendars Net	The site allows you to maintain calendars of events that are of interest to a group of people free of charge. A link to Egroups (also in this section) lets you e-mail the group when new events are posted. Messy to look at, but a clever site from a public-interest group in the US dedicated to improving communications and reducing global warming.	www.calendars.net/	3	2
	FreeDrive	FreeDrive gives you 20 Mb of free storage space so you can get access to your files from any Web terminal when away from your desk. Your data is password protected, but you'll have to pay $4.95 a month if you want secure encryption.	www.freedrive.com/	1	3
	e.groups	A cracking example of free services on the Internet. This one lets you maintain an e-mail list and bulletin board – really useful if you're working with distant colleagues or have a lot of relatives on e-mail. There's also a private chat room available if you're into that kind of thing.	www.egroups.com	2	4

GENERAL SMALL BUSINESSES

RESOURCES		These resource sites provide concrete information instead of just a list of links or thinly veiled adverts.			
	Royal Mail	The Royal Mail site is worth having a quick glance over because it offers a number of useful features including a postcode locator, a database that enables you to track the progress of recorded and special delivery items and a host of other electronic communication services.	www.royalmail.co.uk/ atwork/default.htm	4	3

Sub Topic	Title	Description		Rele-vance	Ease of Use
	The Enterprise Network	Solid but unremarkable effort from the *Sunday Times*. It does contain useful material but is delivered via a text heavy, unimaginative interface. Ask the Expert is worth checking out though.	www.enterprisenetwork .co.uk/clubs/entnet/ entnet/content.fhtml	1	1
	The Business Owner's Toolkit	The tone is slightly more exuberant than the more low-key British sites, but this US-based site is well worth looking at in a spare half-hour. You might want to check out 'Creating your own wealth building plan' for starters…	www.toolkit.cch.com/	1	1
	ICC Information	You have to pay to get the company information and reports that ICC provides, but they offer free samples to show you what you get for your money. It's also a clean and well-organized site.	www.icc.co.uk/	1	1
	Entrepreneurial Edge	A great resource from the non-profit-making Edward Lowe Foundation but not good for culturally specific stuff (eg finance and law) because it is a US-based site. Use it for marketing and less nationally specific information instead.	edge.lowe.org/	2	2
	The Enterprise Zone	The flashing graphics on the home page can't disguise the fact that this UK-government sponsored site is really just a list of links and not even a particularly well-organized one. You might find a useful link amongst them however.	www.enterprise-zone. org.uk/	1	0
	American Express Small Business Exchange	There is a US slant to this site, but the information is wide-ranging and intelligent and the sales pitch is thankfully separated from the information. Good for beginners because of its clear written style and easy-to-navigate interface.	www6.americanexpress. com/smallbusiness/	3	3

Sub Topic	Title	Description		Rele-vance	Ease of Use
	UK Business Net	Don't let the slightly oppressive interface put you off. It may look drab but this is an excellent general UK-based business resource with extensive (although not always reliable) links to a myriad of organizations.	www.ukbusinessnet. com/intro.htm	3	1
	Netscape Netcenter Small Business	Very basic small business e-source site from Netscape.	home.netscape.com/ netcenter/smallbusiness/ index.html	1	1
	UK Business Incubation	There's an excellent A–Z glossary to UK business funding terms on this site, which on its own makes these pages well worth a visit.	www.ukbi.co.uk/	2	1
BUSINESS PLANNING		These are some of the best resources we found in an area where (unsurprisingly) the good-quality stuff is dominated by North American sites.			
	Starting a business: business planning	Useful introduction from US-based company. Luckily some of the more general resources are equally applicable in the UK.	www.businessplans. org/topic21.html	1	1
	The Interactive Business Planner	A clever idea developed by the Canadian government as part of its network of Canadian Business Service Centres. After logging on, the Web site takes you through a step-by-step guide to creating your own business plan. You can save it and finish it off on a later visit. A good example of offering something different and useful on a Web site.	pegasus.cbsc.org: 4000/sbc-doc/home _en.html	3	4
	Planning for a Business Start-up	An academic site geared to students of business studies.	sol.brunel.ac.uk/ jarvis/bola/businesses/ busplan/index.html	2	1
	British Franchise Association	User friendly and unpretentious. This is an essential site to visit for anyone who is thinking about developing their business by taking on a franchise.	www.british-franchise. org.uk/	2	2

Sub Topic	Title	Description		Rele-vance	Ease of Use
	FranInfo	Very similar to the other franchise sites. Databases, guides, news, etc. It is best to plough through them all and pick and choose what you need.	www.franinfo.co.uk/	2	1
	Franchise Direct	Slick production from an Irish-based outfit. Allows you to search for franchise opportunities as well as offering general information and news.	www.franchisedirect. co.uk/index.htm	2	2
DIRECTORIES		A range of directories from general ones such as the Yellow Pages to more specialist databases. Also check out the directories in 'Business essentials'.			
	Companies House	Model Web site, beautifully designed. You can search the database for company information but (strangely) only on Monday to Friday from 8 am to 8 pm.	www.companies-house.gov.uk	4	3
	AskAlex	A fast, efficient, massive database on UK businesses amongst other things. Although the detail supplied is minimal (just phone and address), it is certainly a good alternative to national directory enquiries, mainly because you can browse results if you are not sure about a particular name or location.	www.askalex.co.uk/	4	4
	Yell	The online version of the Yellow Pages is a welcome addition to the world of Web-based directories because it allows you to do national searches unlike its paper counterparts. It also gives access to host of other types of information including weather, entertainment and travel. Highly recommended.	www.yell.co.uk	3	3

Sub Topic	Title	Description		Rele-vance	Ease of Use
	BT PhoneNet UK	When you need to find a phone number it's cheaper to log on to this online service than to call directory enquiries.	www.bt.com/ phonenetuk/	4	3
	BIX-AEC Construction Industry Directory	Directory for those in the building, engineering and construction industries. The entries read more like adverts than directory listings and it is far from comprehensive, but a visit may be worthwhile if you're in the trade.	www.building.org/	1	1
	UK Directory	Another sprawling directory covering a wide range of topics for those of you who just can't get enough of them...	www.ukdirectory.com	2	1
NEWS AND MAGAZINES		Most of the online journals are US-based which means that you have to be quite selective in what you use them for. We have also included some old UK favourites here.			
	Ft.com	Helpful features of this online *Financial Times* Web site include the personalized newsfeeds via e-mail and a portfolio service, but you need to register for these. Access to some areas of the site requires payment after a given period of use.	www.ft.com/	1	3
	Exchange and Mart	Online version of the newsagent perennial.	www.exchangeandmart .co.uk/	1	2
	Bizproweb	You can download business-oriented shareware from this Web site and it contains a rash of business articles from contributors whom we are reassured are 'experts' in their field. However, it is unclear how frequently (if at all) these are changed and the rest of the site is really rather thin (links, links and more links...)	www.bizproweb.com/	1	1

Sub Topic	Title	Description		Rele-vance	Ease of Use
	The Economist	Good for general news browsing when you have an idle moment in front of the computer, but if you want any hard economic data then you need to pay the current £30 annual subscription for the online publication.	www.economist.com/	2	2
	Pool Business and Marketing Strategy	An online business strategy magazine with a pool metaphor carried cleverly right across its design and layout. Worth a peek (for the design 'idea' if nothing else) but the content is slightly thin and it is unclear how regularly new material is added.	www.poolonline.com/main.html	1	2
NATIONAL BODIES		They are usually 'dull but worthy' – nevertheless the Web sites of national bodies are often the best place to start looking when you need to gather information about them. Thankfully some of them are even good Web sites …			
	CCTA Government Information Service	The dense Government Information Service Web site is best visited when you have a specific public policy query to look up.	www.open.gov.uk/	1	1
	Business Link National Site	This site has little information in its own right, although it will make you aware of Business Link services and will also help you track down your local business Link. The clickable map is a good feature.	www.businesslink.co.uk/	1	1
	UK Department of Trade and Industry	Slick (for a government site) and with a lot of useful information.	www.dti.gov.uk/	2	2
	Federation of Small Businesses	A rather dull site which has little to interest the casual visitor. A few headlines, a bit of low-key plugging of their services and a list of offices. Worth going to only if you want more information about FSB.	www.fsb.org.uk/	1	0

Sub Topic	Title	Description		Rele-vance	Ease of Use
	The British Chambers of Commerce	Unexciting but useful for those researching the BCC. There is a members only section.	www.britishchambers.org.uk/index.html	1	1
TRADE ASSOCIATIONS		For when you need to find the trade association for a particular business area.			
	Trade Association Forum	A comprehensive directory of UK trade associations. This is all you need, really…	www.taforum.org.uk	4	2
FINANCE					
TAXATION		They're not all as dull as you might expect.			
	The Chartered Institute of Taxation	A general guide to taxation, which is thoughtfully divided into beginners' and experts' sections.	www.tax.org.uk/	3	3
	Kestrel Taxation Services	This quirky, homespun-looking 'labour of love' site is intriguing because it is packed with 'insider' information on Inland Revenue practice from a former IR inspector now turned tax consultant. Unclear from the site how recently or regularly it has been updated though. Watch out for the music.	www.kestreltax.u-net.com/	2	0
	Inland Revenue	Not the most imaginative site you'll ever see, but it has lots of information on tax issues relevant to small businesses. Being able to download forms is a particularly handy feature.	www.inlandrevenue.gov.uk/home.htm	2	2
ACCOUNTANCY		Most sites are aimed at accountants rather than small businesses.			
	The Official ICAEW Directory of Firms	The Web site of the Institute of Chartered Accountants of England and Wales. It has a free and seemingly well-stocked directory on its site that enables you to search for chartered accountants by location or area of specialism. And it offers worldwide coverage.	www.icaewfirms.co.uk/	2	2

Sub Topic	Title	Description		Rele-vance	Ease of Use
INSOLVENCY AND BANKRUPTCY		These site reviews can also be found in the legal section of the guide since the subject 'straddles' both areas.			
	The Insolvency Service	A clear and accessible guide to bankruptcy geared to company directors who want to know more about this complicated subject.	www.insolvency.gov.uk	1	1
	Personal Insolvency – 20 useful things to know about Individual Voluntary Arrangements	A simple page of text on individual voluntary arrangements that is an alternative arrangement to a formal declaration of bankruptcy. A useful introduction for anyone unfortunate enough to need this information.	www.kaslers.co.uk/ newsletters/personal %20insolvency/text. htm	1	0
	UK Bankruptcy and Insolvency site	Dense, text-heavy site on insolvency that isn't going to win any design awards, but does the job. The FAQ (Frequently Asked Questions list) is a good starting point.	www.insolvency.co.uk/	2	0
CREDIT MANAGEMENT		Credit management Web sites are usually run by firms charging for their services, so you will need to go out and have a look for yourself to decide whether they are worth it.			
	Business Credit Management UK	This general credit management site mostly offers links, but they are extensive links, and there is also news available. The chat room is a lonely place however.	www.creditman.co.uk/	1	1
Equifax		You can access the services of a credit agency such as Equifax via the Internet, and receive their company credit information online.	www.equifax.co.uk/	1	1
FOREIGN EXCHANGE		The Web has a glut of foreign exchange information that we've 'pruned back' here to a respectable cross-section of what you can expect …			

Sub Topic	Title	Description		Rele-vance	Ease of Use
	BBC News: Foreign Exchange	Currency converters, forex reports and general money stuff from the BBC.	news.bbc.co.uk/hi/ english/business/ foreign_exchange/ default.htm	1	1
	Classic 164 Currency Converter	Very comprehensive (some might say complicated) currency converter.	www.oanda.com/ converter/classic	2	1
	Personal Currency Converter	One of the simplest (some might say basic) currency converters around on the Web.	www.xe.net/pca	2	1
BANKING		The Web sites of banks are usually about as thrilling as damp dishcloths. However the arrival of Internet banking is starting to liven up at least some of them.			
	AAA dir Banking Directory	Not terribly well updated and clunky to use, but this site still offers one of the most comprehensive listing of banks (in the UK and all over the world) that we've found.	www.aaadir.com/	1	1
	The Banking Liaison Group	Mostly tedious sales pitch, but there is some useful general information about banking and business finance on this company site. See the section on handling banking disputes and the guide to factoring, for example.	www.bankingliaison. co.uk/	1	1
BUSINESS SUPPORT		We've steered clear of hard-sell sites and concentrated on those that offer free information.			
	Grants and Grant Proposal Writing	Its US origins make some the information in this guide inaccurate for over here, but it still contains sound advice, which makes it worth a look.	www.slu.edu/eweb/ grants.htm	1	1
	Department for Trade and Industry	Good starting point. It has a sector-by-sector guide to business support schemes.	www.dti.gov.uk/ support/index.htm	2	1
	The Information Society Initiative	This well-designed DTI-sponsored site has a series of pages on grant schemes and examples of good practice. Well worth a visit.	www.isi.gov.uk/isi/	2	2

Sub Topic	Title	Description		Rele-vance	Ease of Use
	SMART	Concise details about the government SMART scheme, which aids technological innovation in small businesses. Case studies on successful bids are also available.	www.dti.gov.uk/support /smart.htm	2	1
FINANCIAL MANAGEMENT		There isn't a great deal of relevant material in this area mainly because the US stuff doesn't apply here.			
	Small Business Exchange: Managing your cash	Amex's highly recommended small business exchange site. It features a series of solid and informative articles including this section on how to manage your cash flow. Pose a question to the small business adviser if the information you want isn't here.	www6.americanexpress. com/smallbusiness/ segments/managing _your_cash.asp	2	3
INVESTMENT		These sites will give you information and contacts across the industry.			
Investment	British Venture Capital Association	A text-heavy, unimaginative site from the British Venture Capital Association. Visit it, though, if you are researching this area because they are big players in the field.	www.bvca.co.uk/ BVCA/Welcome.html	1	0
Investment	LevyGee Venture Capital Database	An excellent idea – a searchable venture capital database. It requires registration before you can access the services.	www.levygee.co. uk/LG/VCD/VCD. NSF?OpenDatabase	1	2
SALES AND MARKETING					
RESOURCES		As usual the US sites take the lead in providing the high-quality Web sites. This section contains mainly resources that deal with 'offline' marketing.			
	Center for Business Planning Resources	This is a general business site based in the US, but it has some high-quality resources on marketing of potential use to British audiences, including an excellent article on devising marketing plans.	www.businessplans. org/plan.html	2	1

Sub Topic	Title	Description		Rele-vance	Ease of Use
	Small Business Marketing: Introduction to Marketing	Very basic – good for absolute beginners or for training purposes.	www.bizmove.com/ marketing/m2a.htm	1	1
	Marketing Week	An online version of *Marketing Week* magazine. The site requires free registration.	www.mad.co.uk/MW/	1	2
	JICREG Listings	The Joint Industry Committee for Regional Press Research publishes detailed data about regional newspapers. This very simple site provides direct online access to demographic and circulation data, which is updated twice a year. Much more than just a list of titles.	www.jicreg.co.uk/	3	2
	Marketing UK	A novelty – a really good marketing resource on the Internet that is British! Particularly useful is a downloadable marketing health check – (www.marketinguk.co.uk/hch eck.htm) – a series of questions designed to help you assess the effectiveness of your current marketing practices.	www.marketinguk. co.uk/	3	3
	SmallBizsearch .com	General US small business portal with a marketing section. Many of the links aren't relevant to UK audiences, but 'dip into' the articles because there are some 'little gems'.	www.smallbizsearch. com/marketing/	2	1
	Small Business Exchange: Marketing	High-quality material from this consistently impressive American Express Site.	www6.americanexpress. com/smallbusiness/ segments/marketing .asp	3	3
	Marketing Online	Really aimed at marketing executives but this slick general marketing news site might fill the odd coffee break and is cheaper to access than the paper version.	www.marketing. haynet.com/	1	1

Sub Topic	Title	Description		Rele-vance	Ease of Use
	Entrepreneurial Edge Business Builders	Its US orientation makes some of the material redundant, but this magazine from the Edward Lowe foundation is still one of the best business resources we've found on the Web. It has its own resources on sales and marketing, as well as downloadable documents often excerpted from books.	edge.lowe.org/ resource/bizbuild/	3	2
PUBLIC RELATIONS		A small but perfectly-formed selection follows…			
	CPR Works Publicity Guide	A very simple but nicely done interactive introduction to dealing with the press from a Midlands-based company. It makes good use of the graphic potential of the Web to give tips about press release layout etc.	www.cpr.co.uk	2	3
	PR Web	US based, but the PR Coach link has useful articles posted by public relations practitioners.	prweb.com/prcoach .htm	2	1
	What is Public Relations?	Straightforward guide to the main whys, whats and wherefores of public relations.	www.pr-school-london. com/Resource/ WhatisPR.html	2	1
	Small Business Exchange: Managing Clients and Customers	The emphasis here is on customer relations only, but it is still quite handy.	www6.americanexpress. com/smallbusiness/ segments/managing _clients.asp	1	3
	Media UK Internet Directory	A wise starting point if you need to track down local and national media contacts. The site features a series of searchable databases. You can search by name or region – a clever idea that has been well executed.	www.mediauk.com/ directory	3	3
MARKET RESEARCH		Particularly handy for market researchers is the Web's capacity to store large amounts of statistical data, which can still be accessed for free on many sites.			

Sub Topic	Title	Description		Rele-vance	Ease of Use
	NOP UK	Limited access to survey results across a range of specialist areas, although the format for listing of articles is not simple, to say the least. Useful basic information is freely available and can be used to set you on the right path to buying what you really need.	www.nop.co.uk/survey/department_frame.htm	2	2
	The Economist Intelligence Unit	Comprehensive global information across a wide range of sectors. You must register and enter credit card details to get access to the content of any reports, although a straightforward search facility means you can see whether it's there first.	store.eiu.com/	3	1
	The UK National Readership Survey	Want to know which magazines and newspapers are read by the most people? Topline information is free, giving helpful overviews of particular sectors. Serious data-miners can buy the information and analyse it on their own computer.	www.nrs.co.uk/contents.cfm	2	1
	Office for National Statistics	General census information online. Worth using if you're doing research on a particular market segment or trend.	www.ons.gov.uk/ons_f.htm	2	2
	Government Statistical Service – The Source	The official Web site of the UK government statistical service. From here you can access Statbase, an online searchable facility containing loads of datasets. A handy tool for any market researcher which costs nothing.	www.statistics.gov.uk	2	2
EXPORTING		These sites are all very similar so have 'a dig around' them all and see what you think…			
	The British Exporters Web site	Mainly aimed at those outside the UK looking for British exporters. You can add a basic entry for your company to the British exporters database for free.	www.export.co.uk/frames1.htm	1	1

Sub Topic	Title	Description		Rele-vance	Ease of Use
	UK Now – Japan	This is 'the British Government's official site in Japan', which has been set up to encourage and promote trade links between the UK and Japan. Includes news, useful information for visiting business people and helpful links, in both English and Japanese. Just one of the many useful sites that can be accessed through the Foreign and Commonwealth Office site.	www.uknow.or.jp/	2	3
	Trade Match	A free service matching up importers and exporters. You can register your own company for exporting, or look for import partners abroad. However, it is not made obvious who runs the site, which leaves a slight trail of suspicion over its services, but one can only try it and see…	www.tradematch.co.uk/	1	1
	Trade UK	This government-sponsored site offers the same sort of export/importing database searches as the others in this area.	www.brittrade.com/ tradeuk/	1	1
TENDERING		How to grab a share of government business.			
Tendering	Tenders on the Web	A subscription-only service that aims to provide subscribers with early notification of invitations to tender. Covers public sector purchasing in the EU. A free sample database can be tried out if you register.	www.tenders.co.uk/	2	1
E-COMMERCE					
RESOURCES		A good place to get an initial feel of what e-commerce is about, and whether you should be selling online.			

Sub Topic	Title	Description	Rele-vance	Ease of Use
	The Electronic Commerce Guide	An extensive site with up-to-date feature articles, though its content reflects its US domicile. Good plain introductions to e-commerce topics and a useful jargon buster. The site contains extensive product reviews, which are handy if you are thinking of buying an off-the-shelf package.	ecommerce.internet.com/	2	2
	ZDNet e-business	The part of US publisher Ziff-Davis's huge Web site devoted to e-commerce. The weekly table of the Top 10 best and worst e-commerce sites alone makes a visit worthwhile.	www.zdnet.com/enterprise/e-business/	1	2
	The E-Commerce Dictionary	The author of this very useful glossary of e-commerce speak, Ted Haynes, runs a consulting company in California (where else?).	www.tedhaynes.com/haynes1/newterms.html	2	3
	Web Marketing and E-Commerce	Splendid general resource site, with lots of useful articles and pointers. 20% of the articles are freely available, access to the remainder costs $50 per year, and looks good value. The most comprehensive collection of e-commerce newsfeeds and free newsletters we've seen.	www.wilsonweb.com/	3	4
	Sell it on the Web	An American site geared towards small businesses who are thinking of moving into e-commerce. Good beginners' section, FAQ (list of frequently asked questions) and news section. The UK site at netsavvy.co.uk/index.html seems to be identical.	www.sellitontheweb.com/	2	2
	Internet.Works	Web site of UK-published *Internet.Works* magazine. The lively and informative section on e-commerce is an ideal starting point for beginners.	www.iwks.com/	2	1

Sub Topic	Title	Description		Rele-vance	Ease of Use
	High Tech Advertising White Papers	A clutch of articles written by someone who not only knows their way around marketing online, but also has a good turn of phrase to help keep things very readable. The articles are too long to digest online but then they're also easily printed.	www.pawluk.com/ pages/ marketingj.shtm	2	2
	The Ecademy	A site that's making a real effort to build a community of interest. Free membership gets you daily newsletters, tutorials and invitations to real-life meetings. The open part of the site has a wealth of UK-relevant information.	www.theecademy.com/	4	4
INTERNET MARKETING		How to get people to visit your electronic storefront.			
	The Internet Marketing Centre	US-based site that has a lot of very useful information, ideas, tips and links. Free monthly newsletter is delivered by e-mail and the whole thing has an air of authority, both as somewhere to get started and as somewhere to keep coming back to.	www.marketingtips. com/	2	2
	NUA Surveys	Long-standing Internet-only survey company. Based in Ireland, it compiles results from a variety of sources on a rolling basis. Search the Web site for all sorts of 'goodies', and try the excellent mailing lists to keep a finger on the Internet's pulse.	www.nua.ie/surveys/	4	2
	Link Exchange	A Microsoft-owned site that collects together a number of valuable online resources for starting, promoting and managing your Web site. Includes services for submitting your site to up to 200 search engines at one time, an inspection of your site and several tactics for attracting more of the visitors	www.linkexchange .com/	3	2

Sub Topic	Title	Description	Rele- vance	Ease of Use
		you want. A few things are free but it's all fairly cheap, especially if it keeps the eyeballs coming.		
	Essential Resources for the Entrepreneur	You don't have to look far for lists of sites that will help promote your site. At least this one is both short and contains editorial. It also places value on services that are free, so it's certainly worth a look if you're not sure how much you want to spend.	www. marketingresource.com/	1	1

SUPPLIES AND PURCHASING

DIRECTORIES		These general directories provide lists of vendors' sites on a wide range of products and are often hosted by search engines or ISPs.		
	British Shopping Links	General consumer wares and business products under a wide range of headings.	www.british-shopping .com/	1	2
	Lifestyle UK-business life	A directory with links to a large number of companies selling office products. Lifestyle UK promises that firms included are quality controlled, although the issue of whether you have to pay for an entry remains unclear. Use it if you can't find what you want from any of the other sites listed here.	www.lifestyle.co.uk/ bid.htm	1	1
	The Yahoo! office supplies and services directory	Business directories like this one feature on many search engines but Yahoo is one of the more established ones. Again, remember quality or usefulness is not guaranteed with these listings, so it's best to treat them as an opportunity for a bit of window shopping.	www.yahoo.co.uk/ Regional/Countries/ United_Kingdom/ Business_and_ Economy/Companies/ Office_Supplies_ and_Services/	1	1
	UK Electronics Manufacturers	A DTI-sponsored directory of electronics manufacturers is a good idea. A shame it is underpopulated at the moment but it may take off, so watch this space…	www.electronics.org.uk/	1	1

Sub Topic	Title	Description		Rele- vance	Ease of Use
OFFICE SUPPLIES		The following is a selection of office supplies sites that are well designed and offer online purchasing.			
	Office Shopper	A wittily designed, attractive site from an Oxfordshire-based outfit that allows you to test-drive electronic purchasing before committing yourself to registering or buying. All products are illustrated and the shopping cart system works beautifully. A must.	www.officeshopper. com/	3	5
	Pelikan Ink and Paper Products	Online ordering is not as convenient here as on the better sites because you have to cut and paste reference numbers and not all products are illustrated. Does specialize in ink products though.	www.pelikan.co.uk/	2	1
	Top Copier Products	Sells copiers, plasma displays and laser printer products amongst others. Being able to download detailed product brochures as Acrobat files makes it good for window shopping.	www.top-copier.co.uk/	1	2
	Inkjet Cartridge	The good news is that this firm deal exclusively in Inkjet printer cartridges and paper so it is easy to find what you want. The bad news is that it's delivered via one of the most garish, visually unpleasing interfaces imaginable.	www.inkjet-cartridges.co.uk/	1	0
	Viking Direct	Viking is undoubtedly one of the best examples of an office supplies Web site. Everything is illustrated, the system is brisk and simple to use and they offer free delivery overnight in the UK for orders over £30. A really impressive example of e-commerce working at its best.	www.viking-direct .co.uk/	4	5

Sub Topic	Title	Description		Rele-vance	Ease of Use
	The Office Shop	Clean design and well illustrated, but the shopping system is not quite as intuitive as some of the others, and you can only get free delivery for orders over £100.	www.owa.co.uk/acatalog/	2	2
ONLINE BOOKSHOPS		There are many online book vendors but start off with this one because it is hard to beat...			
	Amazon	The UK site of probably the best-known Internet vendor. Has an easy-to-use search facility and a business section. Wonderfully efficient and excellent value.	www.amazon.co.uk/	3	3

TRAVEL

Sub Topic	Title	Description		Rele-vance	Ease of Use
RESOURCES		The following are general-purpose travel sites that do a variety of things from telling you about visas to giving all-purpose travel information.			
	Foreign and Commonwealth Office	Attractive site from the UK government's Foreign and Commonwealth Office. It includes essential information on visas, country-specific travel advice and how to use consular services abroad. Invaluable for the frequent flier and interesting for the rest of us as well.	www.fco.gov.uk/	3	4
	Virgin Net	An informal, accessible style characterizes this high-quality general travel site from Virgin. Even the discussion board is well used.~	www.virgin.net/travel/index.html	1	3
	Expedia UK	Expedia is Microsoft's general travel site. As well as the usual flight and accommodation searches, there is a section that is aimed at business travellers. You need to register before you can search for flights.	expedia.msn.co.uk/	1	2

Sub Topic	Title	Description		Rele-vance	Ease of Use
AIR TRAVEL		Those miraculously cheap flights have a habit of disappearing when you start checking for availability, but try it for yourself anyway…			
	A2B UK Airport Information	The vital statistics on UK airports – how to get to them, where to park, where you can stay and what facilities they offer. A neat idea that has been well executed.	www.a2bairports.com/	2	3
	Air Miles	Check out how far your acquired air miles can take you by logging on to this smart and well-organized Web site.	www.airmiles.co.uk/	1	2
	Deckchair.com	Another 'cheapie air travel' site that is easy to use and efficient, and you don't have to register straightaway! Use it alongside the other sites to give you an idea of prices, times and availability.	www.deckchair.com/defaultie4.htm	2	2
	LastMinute.com	Geared more to the holiday market and you have to register before you can get times and availability.	www.lastminute.com/lmn/default.asp	1	2
	Cheapflights	The results generated by searches look terribly comprehensive, but it can be slow to check availability and the cheap deals listed are invariably not available on the dates you want. It still might be useful for research nevertheless.	www.cheapflights.co.uk/web/flightlineweb.html	1	2
	Travelocity	You have to register before you can do anything here…	www.travelocity.co.uk/	1	1
DESTINATION GUIDES		The following are no substitute for the convenience of a printed book when you're on your travels, but you can see in advance whether the books are worth buying and use them to do research.			

Sub Topic	Title	Description		Rele-vance	Ease of Use
	Time Out	A series of guides to cities all over the world from the well-known London-based listings magazine. There is a cultural/arts slants to much of their news coverage.	www.timeout.com/	2	2
	Rough Guide	The Rough Guide does not have such a wide coverage of destinations as the Lonely Planet site, but from here you can also access their other online guides including the excellent 'Rough Guide to the Internet'.	www.roughguides.com/	2	3
	Lonely Planet	Definitely geared to backpackers rather than business travellers, the Lonely Planet site has an extensive coverage of countries. It is particularly useful for business travellers going to less-frequently visited countries – even Uzbekistan is comprehensively covered!	www.lonelyplanet.com/	2	3
	CIA Factbook	Economic and social statistics and some rather basic maps are available on this country-by-country reference guide, from the CIA of all people! The amount of information provided here is quite substantial and it is not only good for business travellers overseas, but also for those at home researching potential new markets abroad.	www.odci.gov/cia/ publications/factbook/ index.html	2	1
ACCOMMODATION		This selection is by no means comprehensive but it offers an excellent starting point – well-executed sites that could save you a lot of leg work.			
	RAC hotel finder	This site doesn't seem to have a huge spread across the UK, but it is good looking and easy to use.	www.rac.co.uk/ html/services/ hotelfinder/		

Sub Topic	Title	Description		Rele-vance	Ease of Use
	The AA – Where to stay, where to eat in Great Britain and Ireland	Over 10,000 places to stay in and eat in, a database that can be searched quickly by region, quality and price range. An excellently produced site although catering more for the tourist market than business travellers.	www.theaa.co.uk/ hotels/index.asp	1	3
	Virgin Net Travel Hotel Finder	It throws out an awful lot of results and, after selecting a hotel, you can view maps, local attractions and book online. One of the best we've seen, and it also has lots of general travel information as well.	www.virgin.net/ travel/leisurehunt/ index.html	3	4
PUBLIC TRANSPORT		This is another thing the Net does really well…			
	UK Public Transport Information	An outstanding site that gives information on all the public transport systems (bus, train, coach, ferry, plane) throughout the UK. You can access Railtrack's interactive timetable or even look up bus times on the Shetland Isles should the mood take you …	www.pti.org.uk/	4	4
Eurostar		Eurostar's Web site carries timetables and pricing but sadly no online booking yet.	www.eurostar.com/	1	1

PERSONNEL AND TRAINING

Sub Topic	Title	Description		Rele-vance	Ease of Use
RECRUITMENT		The Internet is stuffed with recruitment agencies and sites geared up to job hunters. It is good for international recruitment drives (or international job hunting) but be warned that at present most sites have a strong IT bias.			
	Guardian Jobsunlimited	Despite its nosy registration process don't abandon *The Guardian* site altogether, because it is an excellent place for media, marketing and IT job hunting. Not so hot for the general small-business sector however.	www.jobsunlimited .co.uk/	1	0

Sub Topic	Title	Description		Rele-vance	Ease of Use
	Jobserve	Only IT jobs are available here, but this site is brisk, efficient and a good example of how a jobs and recruitment Web site should work. No registration is required.	www.jobserve.com/	1	3
	Jobsite	Customized job searches are possible via this impressive site, which sends you details of relevant jobs via e-mail once you have registered. CV mailing and other job-hunting activities are also available. Highly recommended.	www.jobsite.co.uk	3	3
TRAINING		The best training sites provide online resources that actually are resources instead of adverts thinly disguised as resources. Unfortunately such good sites are rather thin on the ground …			
	Training and Enterprise Councils	Really just an electronic brochure, only worth visiting if you want to find out more about TECs or you need to track down your local TEC. The regional offices often have useful information for small businesses on their own Web sites.	www.tec.co.uk/	1	1
	Training Zone's Toolkit	Training Zone's Toolkit has a wealth of good-quality downloadable materials for those running training courses, on a variety of subjects. Many are geared to the non-business sector, but they are still useful and you don't have to pay.	www.trainingzone. co.uk/toolkit/index.html	3	3
PERSONAL DEVELOPMENT		Many personal development sites consist of whacky prose from the sort of serious oddballs who seem to proliferate all over the Internet, but these sites can be good to 'dip into' during idle moments or when inspiration is seriously needed…			

Sub Topic	Title	Description		Rele-vance	Ease of Use
	Mind Tools	Sound advice on time management and problem solving delivered via a basic and easy to navigate interface.	www.mindtools.com/	2	1
	Virtual Presentation Assistant	This is an unassuming but informative little site maintained by the communication studies department of the University of Kansas, which takes you through a guide to public speaking. Well worth checking out should the need arise.	www.ukans.edu/cwis/units/coms2/vpa/vpa.htm	1	1
	Catbert's career zone	Light relief from the creators of the Dilbert comics including the automatic mission statement generator and weekly career tips. To be appreciated on those really bad office days.	www.dilbert.com/comics/dilbert/career/index.html		
	Techniques for Getting Organised	For a 'swift fix' on time management, check out this page taken from the excellent Training Zone Toolkit resource site (www.trainingzone.co.uk/toolkit/index.html)	www.trainingzone.co.uk/toolkit/manager4.html	3	1
	Managing Yourself, Leading Others	Although it is slightly thin on detail and rather basic, this high-energy site is good for when you need to give yourself a serious wake-up call work-wise.	www.srg.co.uk/	1	1
	Small Business Knowledge Base – Personal Skills	Personal development tips delivered in an upbeat tone.	www.bizmove.com/skills.htm	1	1
	Managing Time and Resources – Time Management quiz	Time Management quiz on the American Express small business site, which was uncannily accurate when I used it.	www6.americanexpress.com/smallbusiness/resources/articles/time_management.asp	1	2
PERSONNEL MANAGEMENT		Most of the best stuff comes from across the Atlantic but is (fortunately) equally applicable in the UK.			

Sub Topic	Title	Description		Rele-vance	Ease of Use
	A Guide to Choosing and Using Management Consultants	A simple and helpful guide to hiring and dealing with those slippery and faintly dodgy beings, management consultants. It comes from the Institute of Management Consultancy itself who should about these things.	www.imc.co.uk/a31 using.htm	2	1
	How to Recruit and Hire For Better Results	Impressively huge and sensible guide to hiring staff. This site is from the American-based Edward Lowe Foundation, a non-profit-making organization dedicated to providing resources for small businesses. It is also worth having a browse over its other pages at edge.lowe.org/	edge.lowe.org/resource/ document/htmldocs/ 6442.htm	3	1
	Interactive Hiring Tool from American Express	A brilliant idea that is simple, and more importantly, fun to use. Check out this step-by-step recruitment guide for yourself.	www6.americanexpress .com/smallbusiness/ resources/tools/hiring /intro.asp?aexp_ nav=sbs_segment _hiretool	4	4
	Recruitment and Selection – book extracts	Sound advice on recruitment and HR management, even though it is a blatant plug for someone's book.	www.btinternet.com/ alan.price/hrm/chap8/ ch8-links1.htm# ch8-mar	2	0
	Human Resources Magazine	The online magazine for the Society for Human Resources Management. Despite being an American outfit, it is useful to browse through since it covers subjects ranging from how to cope with downsizing to employee recruitment. Also features a searchable archive of previous articles.	www.shrm.org/ hrmagazine/		

LEGAL

TAXATION		The finance section of the guide also contains material relating to tax issues.			
	The Chartered Institute of Taxation	A general guide to taxation, which is thoughtfully divided into beginners' and experts' sections.	www.tax.org.uk/	3	3

Sub Topic	Title	Description		Rele-vance	Ease of Use
	Kestrel Taxation Services	This quirky, homespun-looking 'labour of love' site is intriguing because it is packed with 'insider' information on Inland Revenue practice from a former IR inspector, now turned tax consultant. Unclear from the site how recently or regularly it has been updated though. Watch out for the music.	www.kestreltax.u-net.com/	2	0
	Inland Revenue	Not the most imaginative site you'll ever see, but it has lots of information on tax issues relevant to small businesses. Being able to download forms is a particularly handy feature.	www.inlandrevenue.gov.uk/home.htm	2	2
COMPANY FORMATION		Use the database-friendly Internet to take some of the leg work out of company formation.			
	Midland Company Services Ltd	This company is a good example of the many company formation services that have sprung up on the Web. It features the usual company formation services and FAQ (Frequently Asked Questions) section.	www.company-services.co.uk/	1	1
	Companies House	Accessing Companies House online is very efficient use of your time. As well as getting access to their database, you can order forms online, and the site is simple to navigate and pleasing on the eye.	www.companies-house.gov.uk	4	3
INSOLVENCY		Insolvency sites abound on the Internet, so make sure you check out the following should the need arise.			
	Personal Insolvency – 20 useful things to know about Individual Voluntary Arrangements	A simple page of text on individual voluntary arrangements that is an alternative arrangement to a formal declaration of bankruptcy. A useful introduction for anyone unfortunate enough to need this information.	www.kaslers.co.uk/newsletters/personal%20insolvency/text.htm	1	0

Sub Topic	Title	Description		Rele-vance	Ease of Use
	UK Bankruptcy and Insolvency	Dense, text-heavy site on insolvency that isn't going to win any design awards, but does the job. The FAQ (Frequently Asked Questions list) is a good starting point.	www.insolvency.co.uk/	2	0
	The Insolvency Service	A clear and accessible guide to bankruptcy geared to company directors who want to know more about this complicated subject.	www.open.gov.uk/ insolv_s/bankrupts/ gbbank.htm#what is bankruptcy'?	1	1
	The Society of Practitioners of Insolvency	An important body in the field runs this site, but it has a faint air of neglect about it. News items are only posted every few months and the typesetting leaves a lot to be desired in places.	www.insolvency.org.uk/	1	0
PATENTS		Some excellent examples of ways of using the Web to get up-to-date information from databases.			
	Copyright Licensing Agency	Everything you might need to know about copyright delivered via a visually dull but easy to use interface.	www.cla.co.uk/	1	1
	The Chartered Institute of Patent Agents	Spartan-looking Web site of the professional body for patent agents in the UK.	www.cipa.org.uk/	1	0
	European Patent Register	The European Patent Register allows you to search for details about patent applications across all European countries. You have to pay to use it but for those who really want to research the progress of a particular patent application it's worth bearing in mind.	www.european-patent-office.org/ epidos/epr.htm	1	1
	The Patent Office	An essential site to visit: it caters for all level of experience from the excellent newcomer's guide to a series of searchable databases.	www.patent.gov.uk/ index.html	3	2

Sub Topic	Title	Description		Rele-vance	Ease of Use
EMPLOYMENT		Be warned that some dedication is needed to plough through some of these horribly dry sites, which are often aimed at lawyers.			
	IDS Employment Law Link	This company provides data on employment issues and via this site they offer large amounts of employment law case studies and EU legislation. Not bedtime reading, but the Web is quite an efficient way of accessing this sort of information should you need it.	www.incomesdata. co.uk/brief/ell.htm	1	1
	Bevans Solicitors	Bevans are a group of solicitors based in Bristol. On their home page go to DIY documents, from where you can access legal letter templates covering areas including breach of contract notice and employee warning. You never know when you might need them…	www.bevans.co.uk/ frames2.htm	1	1
	The National Minimum Wage	Information from the DTI on the legal responsibilities placed on employees by the introduction of the national minimum wage.	www.dti.gov.uk/ir/nmw/	1	1
	Hazards at Work	Government-hosted guide to Health and Safety regulations, which is aimed at employers.	www.open.gov.uk/ hse/pubns/regindex. htm	1	1
	Emplaw	This site boasts that it offers 1,200 pages of free employment law information. That's true, but what you get is acres of dense prose and unless you have a grasp of legal language already, it's difficult to make much sense out of what's in front of you.	www.emplaw.co.uk/	1	0
TECHNOLOGY					
RESOURCES		Use the following sites for technology news, looking up references, and for general browsing in idle moments…			

Sub Topic	Title	Description		Rele-vance	Ease of Use
	ZDNet Small Business Guide	ZDNet are a well-known brand on the Internet and many rate them highly but this site is not great for beginners. As well as being very cluttered visually, much here is geared to the US market. Guides to technology for small businesses feature on the site, and the online small business advisor is a good feature. But use sparingly unless you like being visually over-stimulated or you are a serious technology 'junkie'. There is also a UK ZDNet Web site without the business features available at www.zdnet.co.uk/	www.zdnet.com/smallbusiness/index.html	2	1
	Entrepreneurial Edge Technology	The Edward Lowe Foundation offers a pot-pourri of links, resources and articles on technology use for small businesses. Slightly patchy but still worth a look.	edge.lowe.org/quick/tech/	2	1
	Webopedia	Make this computer and Internet technology dictionary your first port of call when you get 'niggled' by any baffling technobabble. The explanations are in plain English yet accurate, and the site is blissfully free of people trying to sell you things when you're reading about ISDN or whatever…	webopedia.internet.com/	4	2
	Cyberatlas	Cyberatlas takes snippets from market research reports and reproduces them on one Web site. Mainly of interest to those who really want to keep abreast of trends in Internet use and adoption rates. Otherwise all those statistics tend to just merge together and the eyes start to glaze over…	cyberatlas.internet.com/	1	2

Sub Topic	Title	Description		Rele-vance	Ease of Use
SOFTWARE		There are seriously large amounts of high-quality, low-cost computer software available on the Internet, not to mention the acres of free shareware you can download.			
	Software Paradise	Despite its messy opening page, this site goes on to pleasantly surprise with its well-designed and easy-to-use online ordering system for software products.	www.softwareparadise. co.uk/	2	2
	Software Warehouse	Offers the attractive prospect of being able to buy all mainstream PC software and some computers online at discount rates. It really is a warehouse though. The 'no-frills' descriptions are spartan at best, so you really need to know exactly what you want before entering this site.	www.software-warehouse.co.uk/	1	2
	Fileworld	Hours of pleasurable distraction material is available at this shareware Web site run by PC World Online –you can download really useful shareware for your business (like Star Trek Wallpaper or little e-mail programmes) and delude yourself that it's actually work you're doing.	www.pcworld. com/fileworld/	1	2
HARDWARE		Unsurprisingly these Web sites are mostly the efforts of companies desperately trying to sell you things.			
	Information Systems Metalist	Halfway down this mammoth list of links to technology sites compiled by the Engineering department of Washington University is a selection of links to computer vendors. It isn't comprehensive, however, and unsurprisingly there is a US bias to the listings.	www.cait.wustl.edu/ infosys/infosys.html	2	0

Sub Topic	Title	Description		Rele-vance	Ease of Use
	Guide to Computer Vendors	An attractive interface and impressive breadth of listings make this searchable database one of the best we've come across for tracking down computer vendors online.	guide.sbanetweb.com/	3	3
DEVELOPMENT SUPPORT		We have chosen to concentrate here on those sites relevant across the UK small business sector.			
	The Information Society Initiative	This DTI-sponsored site has downloadable documents on new technology written in plain English (excellent for beginners), a series of pages on grant schemes and examples of good practice. Well worth a visit.	www.isi.gov.uk/isi/	3	2
	SMART	A short, simple but useful piece of information – details about the government SMART scheme, which aids technological innovation in small businesses. The rest of the DTI support pages also carry information about other government schemes, so have a browse.	www.dti.gov.uk/ support/smart.htm	2	1
INTERNET RESOURCES		The following are all sites that will help you improve your use of Internet technology.			
	Freeserve Domain Names	There are many companies that advertise domain name registration. Freeserve is tailored to the UK audience and it features a detailed yet simple breakdown of FAQs to help you understand the process. Do shop around before you buy though, because a variety of services are available with a corresponding variety in prices.	www.freeserve.net/ domainnames/ Domain_1.htm	2	2

Sub Topic	Title	Description		Rele-vance	Ease of Use
	Network Solutions	US-based domain name registration service that offers registering and reserving of domain names.	www.networksolutions.com/	2	2
	Register.com	Step-by-step guide to domain name registration is a helpful feature but forcing you to register before you can do anything isn't.	www.register.com/	2	1
	Egroups	A really handy Web site that offers a painless and simple way of setting up an e-mail group. Not only are e-mail groups good in the workplace they're also handy for keeping in contact with business colleagues across the world. And it's free!	www.egroups.com/	3	4
EUROPE					
MAGAZINES		Use the following as material to casually browse through, since they are not very comprehensive in the information they provide.			
	Europages Business Guide	The quality of the information on this colourful magazine site is rather 'hit and miss', but it has some useful links and is geared to the business user.	www.europages.com/business/business-info-en.html	1	1
	Europe Online	Huge, sprawling Web site divided by country and thematically. As an information resource it is rather skimpy but the news coverage is good.	www.europeonline.com/index.htm	1	1
	EU Business	A company Web site that offers large amounts of not-very-well-organized information on EU legislation. It is aimed at business users who want to keep abreast of EU programmes and regulations. A noble idea that could have been better implemented.	www.eubusiness.com/economy/index.htm	1	0

Sub Topic	Title	Description		Rele- vance	Ease of Use
OFFICIAL BODIES		Be warned that most of these are dire and merit inclusion only because of who has put up the Web site and not because of their quality.			
	Europa	A terrible Web site – jargon filled and totally unfriendly to the user. We've only included it because it is the official EU site. Shame on you EU.	europa.eu.int/index- en.htm	1	0
	EU Electronic Information	Direct access to EU databases online. If this is something you have to do, this is a very quick and efficient way of doing it. Just don't expect it to be fun.	eur-op.eu.int/en/ general/b2.htm	1	0
	The European Commission in the UK	European Commission representation in the UK. It's not very easy to locate the information you require on this site.	www.cec.org.uk/	1	0
BUSINESS SUPPORT		These are the best of a confusing and low-quality bunch. Don't expect to be able to make much sense out of them.			
	UK Business Incubation	In the 'glossary' section there is an excellent A–Z guide to different funding terms that covers EU schemes. It is not quite detailed enough, but it will still help you make sense of all the acronyms.	www.ukbi.co.uk/	2	1
	SME specific measures	A detailed outline of funding criteria for small and medium-sized businesses that are thinking of making a funding bid to the EU under the Research and Technological Development programme. Again not very clear or accessible, but if you're researching EU business funding, it is essential.	www.cordis.lu/sme/ home.html	1	0

Sub Topic	Title	Description		Rele-vance	Ease of Use
	Cordis	Cordis is an information service run by the EU that aims to give advice and information to companies on research and development funding bids. The cluttered interface does not help to make the complexities of EU business support schemes any clearer.	www.cordis.lu/	1	0
	UK Network of Euro Information Centres	Their Web site is infrequently updated, and rather dull, but the the UK Network of Euro Information Centres might be able to help you make sense of the European funding maze.	www.euro-info.org.uk/	1	1
EURO		These sites tend to suffer from the same degree of 'Eurobabble' as other more general European sites. Therefore use sparingly and treat with caution.			
	Get ready for the Euro	This UK-government site does not appear to be updated regularly, but it serves as a straightforward and sensible introductory guide to this subject.	www.euro.gov.uk/	1	0
	EmuNet	It has a messy interface and does not make itself attractive to newcomers to this subject. Nevertheless the site is useful for keeping track of developments with the euro.	www.euro-emu.co.uk/index.html	1	0
	Practical Issues arising from the Euro	Fairly specialized, but the Bank of England site is handy in so far as it concentrates on the implications of the euro for the British economy. Offers downloadable documents.	www.bankofengland.co.uk/piq.htm	1	1
	BBC news – The Euro	The most accessible euro site comes from the BBC. It is not primarily geared to the business user but it's an excellent starting point.	news.bbc.co.uk/hi/english/events/the_launch_of_emu/euro_home/default.htm	2	2

Index

money sites   78
Multimap   22

national bodies sites   43, 58,
    84–85
news sites   18–19, 33, 42, 76–77,
    83–84
newsgroups   28–30

Office Shopper   53
office supplies sites   52–53,
    96–97
official bodies sites   43, 58,
    84–85
    Europe   111
one-to-many e-mail   25
one-to-one e-mail   24–25

Patent Office   58, 59
patents sites   105
personal development sites
    101–02
personnel and training sites
    48–51, 100–03
personnel management sites
    102–03
'portal' sites   18–19, 34
post information sites   75–76
public relations sites   90
public transport sites   100
purchasing sites   51–53, 95–97

Railtrack   54, 55
rating sites   3–6

recruitment sites   100–01
reference aids   33
relevance criterion   3, 4, 5
research sites   57–66
    e-commerce   64–66, 92–95
    Europe   59–61, 110–12
    legal context   57–59, 103–06
    technology   62–64, 106–10
resources sites   33, 79–81
    e-commerce   92–94
    sales and marketing   88–90
    technology   106–07
    travel   97

sales sites   45–47, 88–92
search engines   7
searching hints   70–72
selecting sites   3–6
Sell it on the Web   66
small business sites   31–35
software sites   108
'spam'   25–26
star ratings   4–6
supplies sites   51–53, 95–97
Systran   55

taxation sites   85, 103–04
technology sites   62–64, 106–10
telephone information sites
    75–76
tendering sites   92
threshold criteria, establishing
    4
time information sites   75

About Illustra Research

Illustra Research was formed in January 1999 to develop products and services that would make the Internet more effective and easier to use for everyone. Their mission is to put the power of the Internet within easy reach of both novice and experienced users alike.

Located in the Sussex Innovation Centre at the University of Sussex, UK, it is supported by a network of specialists and experts in the UK and the USA who cooperate on specific projects, using the Internet as a collaborative tool. Illustra also employs teams of researchers who surf the Web to locate relevant material. They are managed by Web Editors, who work alongside subject specialists to rigorously evaluate information according to a unique methodology.

The directors of Illustra:

Alan Saunders, Managing Director, has been in the multimedia industry since its birth and has worked on projects for a wide range of blue-chip clients including Hewlett Packard, Olivetti, British Airways, NEC and Panasonic.

Colin Dixon, Technical Director, has worked with computer networking systems and PC technologies for over 15 years.

Alan Cawson, Research Director, is Professor of Digital Media and Director of the Digital Media Research Centre at the University of Sussex. He has been involved with the Web since its birth in 1993, and writes extensively on consumer information technologies.

For further information about Illustra's activities please contact:

Illustra Research Limited
The Sussex Innovation Centre
Science Park Square
Falmer
Brighton BN1 9SB
Tel: 01273 234650
e-mail: info@illustra-net.com

How to Use Your Top 200 CD-ROM

The CD-ROM that accompanies this book runs under Windows 95, Windows 98 and Windows NT4.0. It is a combination of a high-quality information directory and a fully featured Web browser. The information directory is a guide to the Internet, in which relevant sites are identified, and ordered by topic and sub-topic. Each site has been evaluated for relevance and ease of use according to systematic criteria. Integrated with the directory is a Web browser engine, Microsoft's Internet Explorer, providing seamless integration with the Internet. The browser provides all online features of Internet Explorer, so the user is not 'missing' any functions available to users of other browsers.

1 Topic Index One-click access to links organized within topics and sub-topics using drop-down menus which helps users move quickly to the subject area they wish to research.

2 Browser Window The user sees entries in the directory in the browser window, and with a single click can navigate to the relevant Internet site.

3 Toolbar A clear toolbar provides one-click access to key functions, including Back, Forward and Print. A special 'Guide' button returns the user immediately to the directory – saving time and providing instant help when 'lost' on the Internet.

4 Menu Bar A standard Windows Menu Bar contains all the functions of the CD-ROM.

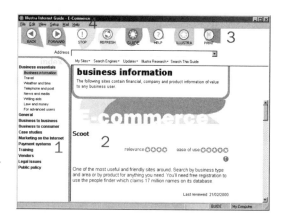

Installation

The CD-ROM installs easily on the user's hard disk. The user can choose where it is installed. Full uninstallation is provided.

Online Update

The Internet is changing all the time as sites appear, change or close down. The CD-ROM includes an update feature, through which users can connect directly to the Illustra Web site, and download an updated version in a matter of seconds.

System Requirements

PC System	Memory (RAM)	16 Mbytes minimum
	Disk Space	20 Mbytes required
	CD-ROM	4x required
	Operating System	Windows 95, Windows 98, Windows NT4.0 (Service Pack 3 or later)
Display	Minimum screen resolution	800x600
	Minimum screen colour depth	15-bit (32768 colours)
Online Requirements	Internet Connection	Windows dial-up or LAN connection to Internet provider
	Modem	Any supported Windows modem
	Microsoft Internet Explorer	Optional. The Guide will supply Internet Explorer functions where IE is not installed, and will upgrade IE versions 1–4 to IE5.